CW00449005

180 YEARS OF
CUNARD

180 YEARS OF CUNARD

CHRIS FRAME & RACHELLE CROSS

FOREWORD BY STEPHEN M. PAYNE, OBE, DESIGNER OF QM2
WITH STORIES FROM CUNARD CAPTAINS, CREW AND GUESTS

The
History
Press

For Zac and Callum

Cover images:
Front: Cunard's flagship *Queen Mary 2* is seen entering Fremantle Harbour.
(Frame/Cross)
Back: *Queen Elizabeth* alongside in Sydney during her 2018 Australian season.
(Frame/Cross)
Page 2: QE2, *Queen Victoria* and QM2 in Southampton in 2008.
(Cunard/Michael Gallagher)

First published 2015 as *175 Years of Cunard*
This edition published 2020
Reprinted 2024

The History Press
97 St George's Place, Cheltenham,
Gloucestershire, GL50 3QB
www.thehistorypress.co.uk

© Chris Frame and Rachelle Cross, 2015, 2020

The right of Chris Frame and Rachelle Cross to be identified as the Authors
of this work has been asserted in accordance with the
Copyright, Designs and Patents Act 1988.

All rights reserved. No part of this book may be reprinted
or reproduced or utilised in any form or by any electronic,
mechanical or other means, now known or hereafter invented,
including photocopying and recording, or in any information
storage or retrieval system, without the permission in writing
from the Publishers.

British Library Cataloguing in Publication Data.
A catalogue record for this book is available from the British Library.

ISBN 978 0 7509 9376 0

Typesetting and origination by The History Press
Printed and bound in India by Thomson Press India Ltd

CONTENTS

FOREWORD

by Stephen M. Payne, OBE RDI

Cunard Line 1840–2020

It doesn't seem like five years has passed since Rachelle and Chris asked me to write the foreword to their book, *175 Years of Cunard*. With the latest edition of the book, *180 Years of Cunard*, I am pleased to write another opening piece. As with any prominent organisation, it is imperative for Cunard to adapt and evolve in order to remain competitive and relevant. As such, the Line has certainly been busy over the past five years.

The biggest event was of course the announcement late in September 2017 that a fourth Queen will be added to the fleet in 2022. Building on the success of the basic *Queen Victoria* and *Queen Elizabeth* platform, itself an enlarged derivative of Holland America Line's successful Vista class, the new ship will be an updated, modified and enlarged version of the previous ships. To be built by Fincantieri like her smaller siblings, the new ship at approximately 113,000 gross tons will be approximately 22,000 tons larger than *Victoria* and *Elizabeth* and carry up to 3,000 passengers. Speculation is rife as to what the name of the new ship will be and what service enhancements and new amenities will be worked into her design.

In the past few years, both the *Queen Mary 2* and *Queen Victoria* have received significant upgrades totalling an investment of US$172 million. *Queen Mary 2* saw the greatest changes, the first really significant upgrade since her entry into service in 2004. In 2016 an additional deck of cabins was added forward, and some public room space was turned over to increasing the cabin count, including the provision of single cabins on board for the first time. Three public spaces saw radical transformations; the rather bland and underutilised Winter Garden was transformed into the vibrant Carinthia Lounge, and the Kings Court casual dining restaurant was completely reimagined with a centralised serving area across the width of the deckhouse. This new arrangement has met with much approval, but it did have one knock on consequence that couldn't be avoided. The Grand Lobby Scenic Elevators, running from the base of the atrium into the old Kings Court arrangement had to be sacrificed as their footprint impinged into what would be the middle of the new centralised servery. Although the loss of the accessibility of the elevators is regretted, their removal has opened up the Grand Lobby in a most spectacular fashion and walking though the space today you wouldn't have imagined that they were ever there. Considering that the *Queen Elizabeth 2* only lasted three years in her original configuration, I believe that the team that created *Queen Mary 2* back at the turn of the millennium did rather well to create a ship that remained essentially original for twelve years. It was certainly a privilege to lead and be part of such a dynamic group. The 2016 reconfigured spaces certainly uplifted *Queen Mary 2* and she resumed her transatlantic schedule and extended winter cruises refreshed and invigorated. I am certainly very proud and a little biased in tendering my opinion that *Queen Mary 2* remains the only true ocean liner in the world and the most capable transatlantic liner in history – especially from a seakeeping perspective.

Queen Victoria's refit took place in 2017, extending her stern upper decks to incorporate additional cabins in a similar fashion to *Queen Elizabeth*'s. The elegant Carinthia Lounge was converted into a single sitting Britannia Club restaurant, echoing *Elizabeth*'s configuration, whilst the Chart Room, Winter Garden and Yacht Club were all refreshed. Meanwhile, after a Cunard absence for more than twenty years, *Queen Elizabeth* inaugurated a short season of ten-day cruises to Alaska from Vancouver during spring 2019. However, the year would also herald another significant milestone, the fifteenth anniversary of entry into service of the venerable *Queen Elizabeth 2*.

It was on 2 May 1969 that *QE2* sailed from Southampton on her maiden voyage to New York at the start of an illustrious seagoing career with Cunard that would last until 27 November 2008. In June 1969, as an enthusiastic 9 year old smitten with ocean liners, I was lucky enough to visit *Queen Elizabeth 2* during a family holiday at nearby Bournemouth as she lay between voyages alongside Southampton's once famous 1950s Ocean Terminal. Memories of that day remain vivid, aided by my father filming us. Bathed in the warm sunshine, Royal Mail Line's elegant *Andes* looked like a graceful swan, whilst lavender hulled Union-Castle liners loaded cargo before passengers in the western docks. Finally, the S.S. *United States* majestically steamed into port on one of her last visits before withdrawal. It just added to the excitement of boarding *Queen Elizabeth 2* for the first time, all new and fresh and already a true style icon. That visit focused my ambition of one day designing her future successor, which ultimately became *Queen Mary 2*. Since 18 April 2018, *Queen Elizabeth 2* has been operating as a luxury hotel and tourist attraction at Dubai.

There is always a sense of excitement when you board a ship. Things are different, especially the terminology: walls are bulkheads, ceilings deckheads, left and right are displaced by port and starboard, floors are decks, and so on. There's much more of course. The sense of relaxation and discovery that's about to unfold during the voyage ahead. Much like this book, which in itself is a voyage of discovery charting the proud history of one of the oldest shipping companies in the world. As we have seen, over the past five years, Cunard has invested and adapted to secure its future with new itineraries, refits and the announcement of a new ship. For my part, I am still as excited today when boarding a ship as I was when I visited *QE2* back in 1969. Certainly, the excitement is all the more when I board one of the present-day Cunard Queens. *180 Years of Cunard* will show you why.

Dr Stephen M. Payne OBE MNM RDI FRINA FREng FRS FSNAME HFIED
Designer Cunard Line Flagship RMS *Queen Mary 2*
Hampshire, England, 4 August 2019

ACKNOWLEDGEMENTS

We would like to thank everyone who has helped us to share the story of Cunard in this updated 180th anniversary edition.

Our thanks go to Stephen Payne for writing an updated foreword for the book. Stephen has been instrumental in securing the future of Cunard Line since he designed *QM2*, and his words are a tribute to both Cunard's past and its future. Thank you also to Captain Aseem Hashmi, Master of *QM2*, who penned a fitting tribute to the 180th anniversary in the afterword of this book.

Thank you to all those who provided us with quotes and stories in both this edition and the 175th anniversary edition, including Andrew Olliviere, Ann Sherry (AO), Anthony Davis, Alastair Greener, Barry Brown, Bill Miller, Captain Ian McNaught, Captain Kevin Oprey, Captain Nick Bates, Carmel Rogers, Caroline Scallan, Christel Hansen, Commodore (retd) Christopher Rynd, Commodore John Burton-Hall, Commodore Ron Warwick, Elaine Mackay, Eli Iniesta, Gaynor van Deventer, Jamie Firth, John G. Langley, Q.C., John Jenkins, Matthew Bambury, Rob Lightbody, Robert Lloyd and Sam Warwick.

We are also very grateful to the photographers, collectors and historians who shared photographic content or assisted us with this book.

Cunard's legendary *Queen Mary* departs Southampton. (Colin Hargreaves)

Once again we send our heartfelt thanks to Ian Boyle for allowing us use of some of his collection of maritime postcards and photographs. He has an extensive collection, some of which can be found at www.simplonpc.co.uk. Our thanks to Michael Pocock, of Maritime Quest, for providing some excellent images. Michael's archive of photographs can be seen at www.maritimequest.com.

We are likewise grateful to maritime historians Rob Henderson and Doug Cremer for access to their impressive Cunard and White Star Line collection used in this book.

We are grateful to Michael Gallagher for providing us with many images for use, including access to his remarkable *QE2* collection and for always being a fount of knowledge relating to all things Cunard.

Our thanks also to photographer Nick Souza who kindly gave us access to the brilliant photographs of *QM2* meeting *Queen Mary*.

Further thanks and acknowledgement goes to Andrew Sassoli-Walker, Andy Fitzsimmons, Bill Miller, Colin Hargreaves, Commodore Ron Warwick, Cunard Line, Elizabeth Williams (Archivist, Cunard – University of Liverpool), Frank X. Prudent, Gavin Harper, George Frame, Jan Frame, Marc-Antoine Bombail, Pam Massey, Rachel Lloyd, Robyn Burn, Ross Burnside, Russell Smith, Ruth Harrington, Tee Adams and Thad Constantine, all of whom assisted us with imagery in both this and the first edition.

And finally, many thanks to Amy Rigg, Tracey Moore, Ian Pearson, Alex Waite and Martin Latham from The History Press for helping us make this book a reality.

Parthia was one of Cunard's many passenger/cargo liners. (Robert Henderson & Doug Cremer collection)

1

THE COMPANY'S BEGINNINGS

Three cheers more and as the first one rings upon our ears the vessel throbs like a strong giant that has just received the breath of life; the two great wheels turn fiercely round for the first time; and the noble ship, with wind and tide astern, breaks proudly through the lashed and foamy water.

Charles Dickens writing of his voyage aboard RMS Britannia *in American Notes*

The first official voyage of the Cunard Line departed Liverpool on 4 July 1840. The ship was the RMS *Britannia* and her crossing to Boston, via Halifax, ushered in a new era in transatlantic shipping. *Britannia* was the first in a quartet of steam-powered paddle steamers built for the Cunard Line and commenced what was to be the first regular transatlantic passenger and mail steam service.

The Cunard Line was originally known as the British & North American Royal Mail Steam Packet Company and was started by the Halifax, Nova Scotia, businessman Samuel Cunard in partnership with Scottish businessmen George and James Burns, David and Charles McIver and Robert Napier. The company was created to operate a mail service between Britain and North America, after Samuel Cunard successfully tendered for the British Government's mail contract.

In the early part of the nineteenth century a mail contract was very lucrative for shipping companies. The contract provided the company with a steady source of income and many of the shipping companies that started around this time relied on the government contract for financial stability. The mail contracts allowed companies to establish a sea route, which could then be expanded to include additional services, such as passenger and cargo transportation.

The British Government had called for tenders for a steamship-operated transatlantic mail service in November 1838, and in 1839 Samuel Cunard travelled to Great Britain to make his bid for the service. On the recommendation of an associate, he engaged the services of Robert Napier, a Scottish shipbuilder, who introduced him to his other future business partners. Napier also worked on the design and build of the first four vessels, which would allow Cunard to complete the requirements of the mail contract.

Britannia was the first of the quartet. At 207ft long, she was a wooden-hulled paddle steamer. The paddle wheels and their machinery took up the majority of the space on board amidships. The cargo hold occupied most of the rest of the space, but, Samuel Cunard, seeing the possibilities, had also instructed builders Robert Duncan & Co. to include passenger accommodation, thus *Britannia* could accommodate up to 115 passengers in a single class.

The accommodation aboard *Britannia* was far from luxurious. Passenger spaces were limited and basic in their design, as per Cunard's instruction: 'I want a plain and comfortable boat, not the least unnecessary expense for show. I prefer plain work in the cabin, and it will save a large amount in the cost.'

As such, passengers slept in bunks, entertained themselves and ate food that was prepared from preserved and dried stores or sourced from the chickens and a cow carried aboard.

Author Charles Dickens, who travelled aboard *Britannia*, described his first view of the ship's grand saloon as a 'long narrow apartment not unlike a gigantic hearse with windows in the sides, having at the upper end

a melancholy stove at which three or four chilly stewards were warming their hands'.

Despite these discomforts, *Britannia* represented a huge step forward for the travelling passenger. Prior to *Britannia* there were few steam ships operating on the North Atlantic. Those that did offer a service, such as Brunel's *Great Western*, offered services in isolation, meaning that the voyages, while scheduled, were not based around a regular timetable (such as a fortnightly sailing).

The other option for those wishing to cross the North Atlantic was to take a journey by sailing packet. Relying on wind power made the sailing journey inherently unreliable; there was no way to guarantee the sailing time and thus it was extremely difficult for shipping companies operating sailing packets to provide a regular service.

This all changed, however, once *Britannia* and her three sister ships, *Acadia*, *Caledonia* and *Columbia*, were in service. With each of these ships having a maximum speed of 9 knots and an average crossing time of

► **DID YOU KNOW?**
....

In March 1849, *Britannia* was sold to the German Confederation Navy and renamed *Barbarossa*. She was later transferred to the Prussian Navy and, in 1880, was sunk whilst being used as a target ship.

Britannia was the first ship built for the Cunard transatlantic service. Here she is depicted aboard *QM2*'s 'Maritime Quest'. (Pam Massey)

fourteen days, Cunard was able to offer a regular schedule, with a ship departing Liverpool once a fortnight.

This made the sending of mails much faster, easier and more reliable. The mail contract had specified the speed the ships needed to make and also the timings of the sailings to be made. If Cunard failed to adhere to these schedules hefty fines were imposed, regardless of whether the company was at fault or not.

Despite the financial implications of any delays, Cunard insisted on a policy of safety over speed with Samuel Cunard giving his captains simple instructions: '... ship, passengers and mail – bring them safely over and safely back'. This policy was to stand the company in good stead for the future.

The Cunard service quickly proved popular and it was not long before Cunard had commissioned a further two ships. The *Hibernia* and the *Cambria* were slightly bigger and faster than the original four ships and held the speed records for their Atlantic crossings. At 219ft long and 35ft wide, they each had the capacity to carry 120 passengers per voyage.

In spite of their safety policy, the Cunard ships were not able to completely avoid the perils of the sea. On 2 July 1843, the Cunarder *Columbia* ran aground in thick fog off the coast of Seal Island. Although the ship subsequently broke up, she was successfully evacuated with no loss of life.

In 1847, the mail contract was renegotiated and the government requested that Cunard increase the number of sailings to have a ship depart once a week from Liverpool, bound for Boston or Canada.

▶ **DID YOU KNOW?** . . . .

Prior to *Britannia* entering service, the steamship *Unicorn* was sent across the Atlantic to Boston by Samuel Cunard. This had the joint effect of creating interest in the new Cunard services, as well as repositioning the *Unicorn*, which was to run a feeder service between Boston and Canada.

Sails were gradually superseded by steam engines, though the early Cunarders retained sails and masts to supplement their steam propulsion. (Frame/Cross)

The new contract was signed and four new ships were built, *Europa*, *America*, *Canada* and *Niagara*.

At over 1,820 tons each and carrying 140 first-class passengers, these ships were both larger and faster than their predecessors. They were also the first ships to use signal lights at night to assist with safe navigation. A red light on the port side, green on the starboard meant that even at night other ships could tell in which direction the Cunarders were travelling. This innovation is still used aboard ships today.

The new ships were also capable of carrying guns in times of war. The requirement to be able to be armed was a stipulation of the mail contracts and signified the government's intent to requisition the ships should the need arise. This was to take effect in 1854 with the outbreak of the Crimean War.

WELCOME ABOARD
QUEEN MARY 2

 Captain Kevin Oprey reflects on taking command of* Queen Mary 2 *for the first time:

Taking Command of *Queen Mary 2* was probably one of the most daunting, exciting and proudest moments in my life. Even to this day, two years after retiring from such an amazing position, it is still difficult to appreciate just how fortunate I was to have held command of a Cunard Line flagship.

I once said in an interview that it is the ship that is paramount. *Queen Mary 2* is far more important than any Captain that has sailed on her in the past, or who will ever be in command on her in the future. A view that I strongly hold to this day.

I consider myself very fortunate that I was one of a relatively small number of Masters who have or will ever have the honour of taking command of a Cunard Flagship. In many ways, it's a private matter, there's a bond that will always exist between myself and the ship and whenever I see her sailing through the Solent, I always feel that part of me is there onboard, sailing with her.

▶ **DID YOU KNOW?**

Sir Samuel Cunard preferred paddle-driven ships to those with screw propellers. He considered them to be safer looking and believed passengers preferred them.

Sir Samuel Cunard, as depicted aboard *QM2*. (Pam Massey)

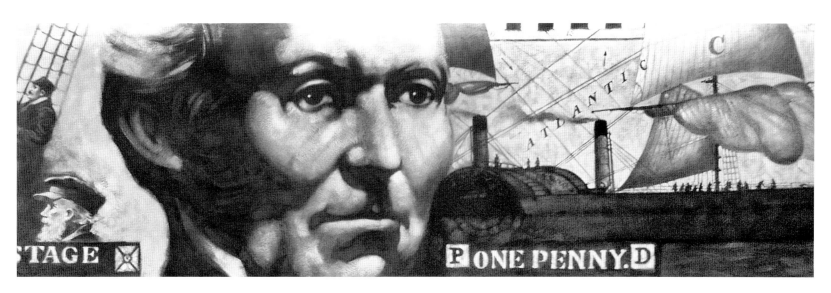

Sir Samuel Cunard and events from the company's history were depicted aboard *QE2* in four murals in her Midships Lobby following the 1994 refit. (Frame/Cross)

Cunard sailing schedule for the 1841 season. (Robert Henderson & Doug Cremer collection)

SIR SAMUEL CUNARD

Born in Halifax, Nova Scotia, on 21 November 1787, Samuel Cunard was the second of nine children. The son of Abraham and Margaret Cunard, Samuel was an exceptionally bright child, displaying high levels of initiative, motivation and entrepreneurship.

Although best known as the founder of the Cunard Line, he had been instrumental in the development and utilisation of steam ships for years before *Britannia* ever took to sea. Samuel married Susan Duffus on 4 February 1815, and together they had nine children of their own. His wife passed away in 1828 and Sir Samuel never remarried.

He was created a baronet by HM Queen Victoria in 1859 for his services to the country, particularly through the Cunard Line and the fleet's invaluable role during both peacetime and war.

After his retirement in 1863, he was succeeded as the head of Cunard Line by his son, Sir Edward, who also succeeded him in the baronetcy. Sir Samuel travelled to Halifax for the final time in the autumn of 1864 aboard the Cunard liner *Scotia*, the last of his paddle-driven transatlantic liners.

On returning to England, his health deteriorated and Sir Samuel died in Kensington on 28 April 1865.

Above: Sir Samuel Cunard, founder of the Cunard Line. (R.W. Warwick; *QE2*: The Cunard Line Flagship *Queen Elizabeth II* collection)

Above right: Deck plans showing internal layouts and engine arrangements for the RMS *Britannia*. (R.W. Warwick; *QE2*: The Cunard Line Flagship *Queen Elizabeth II* collection)

Right: When ice trapped *Britannia* in Boston Harbour, Bostonians freed the ship by digging a channel using shovels and pickaxes. (R.W. Warwick; *QE2*: The Cunard Line Flagship *Queen Elizabeth II* collection)

▶ **DID YOU KNOW?**

RMS stands for Royal Mail Ship.

2
THE EARLY YEARS

The Collins people are pretty much in the situation of finding that breaking our windows with sovereigns, though very fine fun, is too costly to keep on.

Charles McIver to Samuel Cunard

With the advent of the Crimean War, most of the Cunard fleet was requisitioned for war duties, which left the field open for new competitors to grow their own transatlantic shipping companies.

One such company to begin services was the Collins Line. Headed by Edward Knight Collins, the Collins Line commenced North Atlantic steamship services on 27 April 1850 with their 3,000-ton ship *Atlantic*. The Collins Line had obtained a mail subsidy from the American Government on ten-year terms. The subsidy was considerably more lucrative than what was offered to Cunard.

Collins was able to build larger and faster ships that offered far greater luxury than that of the Cunard ships. In addition, he made it a policy for his ships to be as fast as possible. Running the ships at high speed, however, resulted in several problems for the Collins Line; it used more fuel and the increased vibrations led to damage to the vessel, requiring costly repairs.

In response to the competition of Collins Line, Cunard built *Persia* in 1855, their first iron-hulled steamer. *Persia* was able to run at higher speeds, using more powerful engines than any of the previous Cunarders, due to her iron hull. She took both the eastbound and westbound Atlantic speed records from their American rivals in 1856.

Collins Line was not to remain a threat to Cunard for long as a number of disasters ultimately led to the folding of the company. The first such disaster occurred in September 1854, when their ship, *Arctic*, was sunk within 15 miles of the coast after striking another ship in heavy fog. What made this even more tragic for Edward Knight Collins was that his wife, daughter and youngest son were all travelling aboard and were lost with the ship. In 1856, the Collins Line was beset with another tragedy when their ship *Pacific* disappeared during a crossing with all hands.

Despite building a bigger and more luxurious ship, *Adriatic*, to compete for the transatlantic passenger trade, the Collins Line was ultimately unprofitable and was unable to survive the reduction in their government mail contract in 1858.

Throughout Europe there were other new shipping companies opening up, providing continental Europe with steamship connections. Germany produced two strong competitors, with Hamburg-Amerika Line commencing services in 1847 and Norddeutscher Lloyd establishing Atlantic steam ship services in 1857. With the formation of the German Empire these shipping lines became increasingly aggressive in their expansion of transatlantic services.

The British Inman Line had been started in 1850 and although the line did not have a mail contract in the early years, their revolutionary ship, *City of Glasgow*, was designed specifically to undertake voyages in an economical manner. To achieve this, the ship was completed with an all-iron hull and used the more efficient screw-propeller, rather than paddle wheels, making her cheaper to run and maintain.

Cunard responded to the various challenging lines by building new ships. In 1862, *Scotia* entered service. *Scotia* was to be the last of Cunard's record-breakers to be built with paddle wheels. She had an iron hull and was built on similar lines to their ship *Persia*. *Scotia* was larger than *Persia* and faster, eclipsing her speed records.

▶ **DID YOU KNOW?**
. . . .

Prior to *Servia*, it was widely believed that it was too dangerous to use electricity aboard ships.

Edward Knight Collins, one of Cunard's earliest rivals. (R.W. Warwick; *QE2: The Cunard Line Flagship* Queen Elizabeth II collection)

Britannia was a twin-paddle, steam-powered vessel. (Robert Henderson & Doug Cremer collection)

Film historian Barry Brown was a regular lecturer aboard the Cunard fleet, having spoken on all of the modern Queens as well as **Caronia:**

As a film historian, I lectured from 2001 to 2012 on QE2, Caronia, QM2, Queen Victoria and Queen Elizabeth, visiting many interesting countries but, as I live in London, I sailed mostly from Southampton. Ah, such fond memories.

On QE2 one sunny morning at sea, on-board guests were gathering in the ship's cinema for my 11.15 a.m. lecture on 'The Life and Career of Hollywood's Leading Lady – Bette Davis', whom I had met twice as a BBC TV producer of cinema programmes. At 11.10 a.m. the captain made an announcement that, although the ship was not due to dock in Gibraltar until 12.30 p.m., there was a magnificent view of the island right now from the promenade deck. I'm grateful to those five people who stayed to hear my lecture!

In October 2008, I accepted an offer to lecture on QM2 from Southampton–New York–Southampton (twelve days) – little did I know that it coincided with the final transatlantic crossings of QE2. For hours and hours, I watched the smaller QE2 sailing in tandem with QM2, only 1 mile apart. One day it would sail on the port side of QM2, the next day on the starboard side, elegant and graceful. It was joyous to watch this old liner glide across the Atlantic Ocean. The return voyage, both ships departed together from New York, was memorable as QE2 was given a tremendous send-off. I must have been the only traveller who had boarded the ship unaware of the forthcoming historic event.

My favourite lecture venue on any ship is the 'Illuminations Theatre' on QM2, seating 500, each with a good view of the stage. For me to stand, talking to a packed audience with standing-room only was quite thrilling, especially the rapturous applause at the end. It wasn't like that every time but when it did occur, the adrenaline rush was overwhelming. However, jet lag can sometimes be a problem after a long flight to join the ship. On one occasion, I had invited my Australian cousin Christopher to join me on the Sydney–Hong Kong leg of QM2's 2011 world voyage. My lecture on the Australian-born film star Errol Flynn was scheduled for 3.30 p.m. in the Illuminations Theatre. After lunch I decided to have a short nap before getting dressed for my lecture, so my cousin went on deck to catch some sun. He returned to the stateroom at 3.05 p.m. to find me in a very deep sleep. I have never given such a slow, dreary lecture in my life. I wonder if the audience noticed because the positive reception I received was, to my mind, unwarranted.

On the small 24,000-ton Caronia I visited the Faroe Islands and Iceland's capital Reykjavik for the first time, two unique ports of call. Another unique feature on Caronia was the classless one-sitting-only dining room, so unlike the current Cunard fleet.

My first lecture on Queen Victoria, in 2008, was a revelation because the stunning Royal Court Theatre, where the lectures were held, was a replica of a Victorian theatre on the Isle of Man. The technical facilities were excellent and the well-trained crew was reliable and helpful. It was a joy. I lectured on this magnificent ship regularly until April 2011, when I went on a nostalgic Mediterranean voyage to Venice.

In October 2010, I felt honoured to be invited as a lecturer on the maiden voyage of the latest addition to the Cunard fleet, Queen Elizabeth. I was chuffed when I gave the first ever lecture on this wonderful vessel, more or less a replica of Queen Victoria but with an art deco decor.

My final voyage with Cunard was on Queen Elizabeth, from Southampton to Athens, in September 2012. I had been diagnosed with Parkinson's disease, I was 82 years old and I knew it was time to stop. I could not have ended my career on a better ship. I gave six movie lectures, the final one being 'Hollywood's British Gentleman – David Niven'. It was the best of all, just like Cunard.

Cunard's rampant gold lion is still used after 180 years. (Robert Henderson & Doug Cremer collection)

Collins Line's *Atlantic* was larger than its Cunard rivals. (R.W. Warwick; *QE2*: The Cunard Line Flagship *Queen Elizabeth II* collection)

Also entering into service in 1862 was Cunard's *China*. *China* was the first single-screw ship built for the Cunard Line. She was built by Robert Napier & Sons in Scotland and began service on the Liverpool–New York route in March 1862. This ship was unique among the Cunarders at the time of her introduction, in that she was the first to be built with steerage passengers in mind. Steerage accommodation became extremely important throughout the latter part of the nineteenth and early twentieth century. Immigration from Europe to the United States of America was a significant source of income for shipping lines, with millions of people moved by the transatlantic liners during this period.

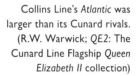

▶ **DID YOU KNOW?**

During her maiden voyage in 1883, Cunard's *Aurania* suffered a major incident when her engines exploded. Fortunately there was no loss of life.

In 1871, the first ship for the White Star Line, the *Oceanic*, entered service. *Oceanic* ushered in a new era of steamship design. With her lavish first-class accommodation placed amidships to reduce movement, she offered passengers a level of comfort not previously seen on the Atlantic.

White Star Line, the brainchild of Thomas Ismay, grew rapidly. A series of agreements saw the line provided with ample capital and the use of the Harland & Wolff shipyard in Belfast, which meant that White Star ships were built in record times, at cost plus a fixed percentage. Such lucrative terms were not available to the Cunard Line.

The year 1871 also saw the American Line commence operations, and the Inman Line introduce a new liner, *City of Brussels*, which eclipsed *Scotia* to become the fastest ship on the North Atlantic.

In response, Cunard built new tonnage and integrated a series of innovations into their fleet. To this end, Cunard's 1874-built *Bothnia* and her sister ship *Scythia* introduced the first dedicated ladies-only lounge, an on-board library and an indoor smoking room. *Bothnia* and *Scythia* were also the first transatlantic liners to employ electric bells, used by first-class passengers to summon their cabin attendant.

In 1876, the mail contracts expired and the new contracts were awarded. Cunard now held only one mail contract, with the others going to Inman Line, Norddeutscher Lloyd and Hamburg-Amerika Lines. To raise capital in the new operating environment, the company reorganised as a publicly listed company in 1879 and was officially renamed as the Cunard Steamship Company Ltd.

In 1881, Cunard was able to launch their first steel-hulled steamship, the *Servia*. *Servia* was the largest ship in service at the time, and second only to the by now retired *Great Eastern*. *Servia* was followed by three iron-hulled vessels, the *Catalonia*, *Pavonia* and *Cephalonia*. These three ships each included accommodation for 200 first-class passengers and 1,500 third-class passengers as well as having the ability to carry cargo.

Passage by steamship in those early years was sometimes dangerous. (R.W. Warwick; QE2: The Cunard Line Flagship *Queen Elizabeth II* collection)

John Langley, QC, is the chairman of the Cunard Steamship Society:

Shipping lines have come and gone over the past few centuries ... longevity was not a common characteristic ... many foundered in a comparatively short period of time, often as a result of horrific losses of ships and passengers on the transatlantic crossing.

Cunard Line is the exception. 180 years after its founding by Halifax native Samuel Cunard, his company is still making history on the North Atlantic and around the world. Its incomparable record of safety and seamanship remains intact, never to be equalled nor surpassed.

As a native 'Haligonian' and Cunard historian, I am very proud to share the same birthplace with the man whose perseverance and old-fashioned hard work has produced the most enduring and famous ocean-liner firm in maritime history.

May the name 'Cunard' and the instantly recognisable burnt-red and black funnels continue to be seen afloat ... making yet more history, for many more years to come.

THE CUNARD ROYAL MAIL STEAMSHIP "BRITANNIA" (John Hewitt, Commander.)
As she appeared leaving her Dock at East Boston, February 3d, 1844, bound from BOSTON to LIVERPOOL, a Canal having been cut in the Ice 7 miles long and 100 feet wide.

Above: The iron-hulled *Persia* was built by Robert Napier and Sons. (R.W. Warwick; *QE2: The Cunard Line Flagship Queen Elizabeth II* collection)

Above right: The *Britannia* is freed from the ice in Boston harbour. (Robert Henderson & Doug Cremer collection)

Right: Early Cunard deck scenes give a sense of the formality aboard. (Robert Henderson & Doug Cremer collection)

 DID YOU KNOW?

Commodore R.W. Warwick was instrumental in the creation of a permanent monument to Sir Samuel Cunard in Halifax, having suggested the idea after *QM2*'s 2004 maiden visit. It was unveiled by the Halifax Foundation in 2006.

Oregon was one of the few Cunard steam vessels that did not have an 'ia' name. (R.W. Warwick; *QE2: The Cunard Line Flagship Queen Elizabeth II* collection)

Catalonia was an iron-hulled ship and entered service in 1881. (Robert Henderson & Doug Cremer collection)

3

STAYING ON TOP OF THE COMPETITION

… in every way, excellent.

The single sentence dedicated to steerage in Cunard's 108-page brochure
for Lucania and Campania

In 1884 and 1885 Cunard introduced two new express liners, *Umbria* and *Etruria*. The largest liners then in service, they were able to achieve a top speed of 19.5 knots thanks to their powerful reciprocating engines and single-screw propellers. Both vessels carried auxiliary sails, the last Cunard ships to do so. These ships introduced refrigeration to the transatlantic trade, which removed the need to carry livestock aboard. Not only did *Umbria* and *Etruria* offer passengers a greater choice of meals, but also a vastly improved smell aboard.

Cunard was not to remain at the top of the game for long, however. Inman Line introduced their twin-screw ships, *City of New York* and *City of Paris*, in 1888, while White Star Line had plans for their own twin-screwed ships, with *Teutonic* entering service in 1889 and *Majestic* in 1890. The twin-screw ships were both faster and more reliable than the Cunard duo and Cunard's express service soon required updating again to get back to the peak position. That was to happen with Cunard's first twin-screw vessels, *Lucania* and *Campania*, which were launched in 1893.

Campania and *Lucania* were built by the Fairfield Shipbuilding and Engineering Company, Scotland. At the time, this yard was one of the biggest suppliers of Royal Navy warships. As with many of the Cunard ships that came before them, *Campania* and *Lucania* were built to government specification, with some of the funding for their building being provided by the British Government.

Both ships were designed for speed, with enormous triple-expansion engines that spanned three decks. Their giant engines produced 31,000hp, which gave them a service speed of 22 knots and allowed them to complete a transatlantic crossing in under six days. *Campania* entered service in April 1893 and captured the Atlantic speed record from Inman's *City of Paris* on her second crossing. *Lucania* took the record from her sister ship the following year, holding the record until 1898.

In addition to being the fastest ships on the Atlantic, *Campania* and *Lucania* were also the largest, most luxurious and some of the safest vessels at sea. Each ship was an impressive 12,950 gross register tons (grt), with furnishings

'

Broadcaster Anthony Davis has always had a love of ocean liners and is a regular aboard the Cunard fleet:

For me, Cunard is about transatlantic crossings, reliving the golden age and reminding ourselves what life was like before jet air travel; before time was of the essence.

I first travelled on *QE2* in 1975, cruising from Southampton to Tenerife and Madeira. I was just 6 months old and was the youngest passenger on board. When I boarded for the second time, in 1983, for a transatlantic two-way crossing, I could remember where everything was. It was like an out-of-body experience. We got

caught up in the infamous storm of '83, off the Bay of Biscay. At the age of 9, I was excited by the vast swells, waves and smashing windows of the Double Down Room.

Nearly twenty years later, I travelled on all three maiden transatlantic crossings on board *QM2*, *Queen Victoria* and *Queen Elizabeth*. Whilst the handcrafted woods have been replaced with synthetic anti-flammable materials, and the clientele may lack the etiquette and class of yesteryear, there is still something magical about a long, slow ocean crossing where you can feel completely alone, amongst your thoughts, without the distraction of Wi-Fi – and have enough time to consume six delicious meals a day.

'

that included Persian carpets and velvet drapes. Their first-class drawing rooms were 60ft by 30ft and their first-class dining room could seat 430 guests in style.

To ensure the reliability of these ships the engines were located in separate, watertight compartments. This allowed Cunard to do away with auxiliary sails; though the masts remained as they performed other functions, including housing crane hooks, flying signal flags, and providing a vantage point for lookouts. As well as the watertight compartments for the engines, the ships each had sixteen transverse watertight bulkheads, with each ship able to stay afloat in the event of any two compartments being flooded.

These safety measures were important in case the ships were ever called up for military service. In the event of damage or flooding to one engine, the other would be able to remain in service, hopefully allowing the ship to continue to make way under her own steam.

In 1901, *Lucania*, *Campania*, *Umbria* and *Etruria* were fitted with Marconi wireless technology. It was now possible to send messages to other ships and to shoreside when in range. This was a huge step forward in terms of safety, but it also introduced new entertainments for the passengers aboard. Cunard ships introduced the *Cunard Daily Bulletin*, a daily newspaper for those aboard that outlined communications between

the ship and other wireless stations. This helped to reduce the feeling of isolation for those aboard and also provided some amusement.

Etruria made use of her auxiliary sails in 1902 when her propeller shaft developed cracks whilst at sea. She was rigged and sailed to a nearby ship that towed her to the Azores for repairs.

Umbria had her own moment of drama in 1903, when a tip-off led the police to discover an explosive waiting to be loaded on to the ship. The bomb was defused and the ship made way without any damage.

Etruria and her sister *Umbria* had a single-screw propeller and auxiliary sails. (Michael Pocock/Maritime Quest)

Umbria (pictured) and *Etruria* were larger and faster than their predecessors. (Robert Henderson & Doug Cremer collection)

All Cunarders carried a cat to take care of any rats. (Robert Henderson & Doug Cremer collection)

Lucania was a new breed of Cunarder, running on twin screws. (Ian Boyle/Simplon Postcards)

Lucania and her sister *Campania* didn't require sails and had oversized funnels. (Ian Boyle/ Simplon Postcards)

This artist's impression of *Campania* shows her looking far larger than the sailing ships and tugs. (Ian Boyle/Simplon Postcards)

Campania and *Lucania* consecutively held the transatlantic speed record, both eastbound and westbound. (Ian Boyle/Simplon Postcards)

This period postcard shows *Campania* along with her general statistics and the Cunard flag. (Ian Boyle/Simplon Postcards)

▶ **DID YOU KNOW?**

Marconi wireless was invented in 1894 by 20-year-old Italian scientist Guglielmo Marconi.

Above: The funnels of *Campania* (pictured) and *Lucania* were the largest in the world. (Michael Pocock/ Maritime Quest)

Left: *Campania*, as depicted on a period postcard, during a busy port day. (Ian Boyle/Simplon Postcards)

Left: *Saxonia*'s single funnel and four masts were common traits on liners of her era. (Ian Boyle/Simplon Postcards)

▶ **DID YOU KNOW?**

Lucania caught fire while in Liverpool in 1909. Despite initial plans to refurbish her, it was decided the damage was too great and the ship was scrapped.

Saxonia in a period postcard symbolising 'hands across the sea' between the United States and Britain. (Ian Boyle/Simplon Postcards)

This artist's impression sought to emphasise *Saxonia*'s bulk. (Ian Boyle/Simplon Postcards)

Above left: An artist's impression of Cunard's 14,280-grt *Saxonia*. (Ian Boyle/Simplon Postcards)

Above: *Albania* (7,640 grt) made her maiden voyage on 17 September 1901. (Ian Boyle/Simplon Postcards)

Left: The first class dining room aboard *Umbria* was a luxurious space when the ship entered service. It featured banquet tables with fixed swivel chairs and electric lighting. (Robert Henderson & Doug Cremer collection)

4

GETTING THERE FASTER

I have come to the conclusion that gearing between engines and screw shafting
will be essential.

Charles Parsons

With so many competitors all challenging for supremacy on the North Atlantic Ocean it was inevitable that Cunard ships would be overtaken in size, speed and luxury. In the final years of the nineteenth century and early years of the twentieth century a number of ships were launched by Cunard's German rivals that took the records from the Cunard liners.

Kaiser Wilhem der Grosse was launched by Norddeutscher Lloyd in 1897. The following year, she became the first German liner to take the westbound speed record. At 655ft long and more than 14,000 grt, she outstripped Cunard's express liners *Campania* and *Lucania*.

She was in turn outdone by Hamburg-Amerika's *Deutschland*, which entered service in 1900 and proved faster and more luxurious than her rival. At 16,502 grt and 680ft in length, she was also larger. Norddeutscher Lloyd responded by introducing *Kaiser Wilhelm II*, which commenced her maiden voyage on 14 April 1903. Bigger still than the *Deutschland*, she was 706ft long and 19,361 grt.

The size and scope of the German liners was not the only concern for Cunard. The White Star Line had commenced a building programme of their own, which introduced their 'Big Four' into service. The first ship in this class was the *Celtic* in 1901. At 20,904 grt, she became the biggest passenger ship yet constructed, eclipsing Brunel's infamous white elephant, *Great Eastern*. The next two ships in the class, *Cedric* (1902) and *Baltic* (1903) were larger still.

This left Cunard in a quandary. The line was not in a strong financial position at the time, though they had managed to resist a purchase attempt by American financier J.P. Morgan in the early twentieth century. Morgan had acquired a number of Cunard's rivals, including White Star Line and the American Line (which had absorbed the Inman Line in 1893), and these companies, along with many others, were re-organised into the International Mercantile Marine Co. (IMM Co.). To make matters worse, IMM Co. had created an alliance with the German lines, adding further pressure to Cunard's bottom line.

Cunard wanted to build two new large express liners to challenge the supremacy of the German and White Star ships, but their finances delayed this process. While attempting to secure funds for their proposed new builds they turned their attention instead to building two 19,500 grt liners.

Carmania and *Caronia* were built at the John Brown Shipyard in Clydebank. They were near identical and ushered in a number of new design features. Both ships were built with high sides and their funnels were painted in different proportion to previous vessels. But the biggest difference between the two was mechanical and therefore not easily visible to passengers.

Caronia was fitted with reciprocating engines. These were the most powerful of their type – eight-cylinder quadruple-expansion engines. *Carmania* was fitted with Parsons Turbines and was the first of the Cunard vessels to use this technology.

The Parsons Turbine was invented in 1884 by Charles Parsons. He had proved the ability of the turbine to propel a vessel by fitting it to a boat named *Turbinia*, and sailing it through Queen Victoria's naval review in 1897. *Turbinia* easily eclipsed the speed of the naval vessels. Parsons' cheeky gamble paid off, with the navy entering discussions with him and soon afterwards beginning to power their new-build ships with this technology.

Merchant shipping was a little slower to catch on. Though aware of the possibilities the new technology provided, it was a great investment for the shipping companies to retrain their engineers to ensure optimum operation of the turbines. In building two near identical vessels each powered by a competing technology, Cunard was aiming to confirm their decision to power their future express liners with turbines.

▶ **DID YOU KNOW?**

Lusitania and *Mauretania*'s names are longer when compared to earlier liners. This was done as Cunard felt their size and scale deserved an extra syllable.

Carmania proved that turbines were more economical than reciprocating engines. (Ian Boyle/Simplon Postcards)

It didn't take long for *Carmania* to prove the case for the turbine. Having entered service in 1905, on the Liverpool to New York route, *Carmania* quickly showed that she was able to achieve greater speeds with less fuel. Though she was not a record-breaker she had proved an important point to Cunard. As a result, Cunard were confident in adopting the turbine technology for their subsequent new builds.

But, in order to become truly competitive on the North Atlantic again, Cunard knew they needed to build new express liners that could recapture the speed record and the attention of the public. The British Admiralty was to assist in this matter.

With Cunard being the last of the large British-owned transatlantic shipping companies, the Admiralty was keen to ensure that they remained competitive and viable, as well as ensuring that a British line was able to challenge for the Atlantic speed record. As a result, they agreed to give Cunard financial assistance to allow them to build what would become known as their 'Ocean Greyhounds'. The conditions of the financial assistance were that the two ships would be very fast – able to achieve speeds of 24 knots – and that they would be able to be converted into armed merchant cruisers if ever the need arose.

WHITE STAR LINE.

TWIN-SCREW R.M.S. "CELTIC."
21,026 TONS.

White Star Line's *Celtic* was the largest liner in the world, which made her popular with transatlantic travelers. (Ian Boyle/Simplon Postcards)

With a loan of £2,600,000, Cunard laid down two new vessels: the *Mauretania* at Swan Hunter & Wigham Richardson in Newcastle and the *Lusitania* at the John Brown shipyard in Clydebank. Both yards were given the same general schematic but were encouraged to compete with each other to build the better ship.

The result was two ships that were vastly different in some ways, yet very similar in others. In external appearance the two ships had very similar hulls, with the main difference being in the location and design of their on-deck air vents and their bridges. *Mauretania* sported large scoop style vents, whereas *Lusitania* was completed with much more streamlined vents. *Mauretania*'s bridge front was larger and bulkier than that aboard *Lusitania*. This gave *Mauretania* a more commanding profile and *Lusitania* a sleeker profile.

Both ships were fitted with turbines as their propulsion system; however, when *Lusitania* – which was completed first – began sea trials it was discovered that the turbines caused significant vibrations at high speeds. *Lusitania* was returned to the shipyard and fitted with additional strengthening beams and *Mauretania* was also completed with the same design. In addition, the propellers were redesigned in an effort to reduce vibrations.

Norddeutscher Lloyd,
Bremen.

Left: The Kaiser-class *were* the first of the four-funnel liners and eclipsed Cunard's speed. (Ian Boyle/Simplon Postcards)

Below left: First class accommodation aboard *Caronia* and *Carmania* was of a high standard, none the less most passenger cabins still didn't have private bathrooms. (Robert Henderson & Doug Cremer Collection)

Below: The steam turbine was a revolution in engineering, saving fuel, time and maintenance. (Robert Henderson & Doug Cremer Collection)

> **Gaynor van Deventer worked aboard the Cunard fleet for many years in the ships' ocean bookshops:**
>
> Growing up partly in Durban, I can recall seeing the Union Castle ships sailing in and out of the harbour as well as *QE2* in Cape Town on 10 November 1970. It was a huge thing for our family to see this vessel – as she was famous, even in South Africa – though we knew we would never be able to afford to travel on her. I then dreamt of one day being able to sail on a ship, never thinking that it would be as a crew member. A few decades later, I was fortunate to secure a position on *QM2*. It was absolutely mind-blowing to step on board the vessel for the very first time; I was dumbfounded by the elegance and stature she presented. I enjoyed working on *QM2* for two and a half years. During this time I met a few celebrities. I was on board *QM2* and witnessed the meeting up with *Queen Mary* in Long Beach California – what a memorable occasion that was.
>
> I changed position and changed ship. The *QE2* was to be my home for the last two years of her career. This was a dream of four decades that finally came true; I was not just looking and admiring this magnificent vessel from a distance, but actually boarding her in Fort Lauderdale as a crew member. I could only understand what I had been hearing about the *QE2* once I set foot on her myself; she had a totally different feel, homely warmth, even though she was older and her interior was not as modern as the *QM2*. She still had her own classic grandeur. In a way it was like stepping into a movie. I was on board when she did her final world voyage in 2008, and I also was present when
>
> HM Queen Elizabeth came to say her last goodbye in June 2008. I left *QE2* in July 2008 to join her new sister, *Queen Victoria*. I had the honour of working with Captain Ian McNaught and there I got to meet many of our repeat guests, and currently still get to see some of these guests who are now sailing on the current Queens.
>
> I must confess, it was very different to come to a brand new ship again. I was glad that I did not do the final trip on *QE2*, as even in the short while that I was working on her, I grew to love her and it saddened me to know that we are not going to have her in the fleet for too much longer. I saw heart-wrenching moments when guests said their last goodbyes, even if it was six months before she was retiring. The final voyage sold out in record time. I have since mainly been sailing on *Queen Victoria*; I have had a very short while on *Queen Elizabeth*, and have been back on *QM2* for the odd cover, but do enjoy *Queen Victoria* at the moment. I have had the honour of working with Commodore Ron Warwick on *QM2* and I have also been on board for many of the special occasions when the three Queens have met up and on 5 June 2012, during the Diamond Jubilee celebrations, I was on *Queen Victoria*. I had a brief stay on *Queen Elizabeth* and it was a bit like déjà vu, so familiar yet so different from *Queen Victoria* was she.
>
> I am very grateful that I got a chance to experience what I once could only dream of. Cunard Line is unique in the sense that even though we are present day, we do still enjoy the pleasures of traditional British lifestyle, afternoon teas, formal evenings, baked Alaska. When the guests are all dressed in true formal attire, it is so beautiful and almost takes one back in time again.

Internally the ships' decor differed. *Lusitania*'s interior was light and bright, making extensive use of plasterwork. The first-class accommodation was completed largely in a Louis XVI style, while second-class mirrored first-class, albeit on a smaller scale.

Mauretania was completed in a quintessential Edwardian style and extensive dark wood panelling throughout. The ship relied on electric lighting to illuminate her darker public rooms, while the first-class dining room was completed in a Francis I style.

Both ships were able to meet their speed targets, with *Lusitania* first, and then *Mauretania* winning the Blue Riband for their crossings. *Mauretania* went on to hold the speed record from 1909 to 1929 with a time of four days, ten hours and fifty-one minutes.

The two ships proved very popular with the travelling public and were able to recapture Cunard's place in the market. They were not to remain the most luxurious liners on the North Atlantic for long, however. In 1910, White Star launched the first of the Olympic-class liners. *Olympic* and her sister ship, *Titanic*, ushered in many new luxuries including a Turkish bath, squash court and opulent parlour suites complete with private balconies.

Despite their speed, *Lusitania* and *Mauretania* were unable to complete a weekly transatlantic schedule; thus, Cunard required a third ship for their express service. Rather than build another ship along the same lines as their 'Ocean Greyhounds', they instead opted to build a slightly larger and more luxurious (albeit slower) ship to compete directly with White Star in terms of luxury.

Aquitania was laid down at the John Brown Shipyard in December 1910. Before she was completed, the sinking of White Star Line's *Titanic* on her maiden voyage shocked the world, leaving lasting changes to the shipping industry. Having struck an iceberg on 14 April 1912 at 11.40 p.m., *Titanic* sank early the next morning with a considerable loss of life.

Cunard's liner *Carpathia* rescued all survivors of the *Titanic* disaster. An intermediate liner that had been built in 1903, *Carpathia* was renowned for her excellent accommodation, the ship's interiors being superior to many other liners.

Immediately following the loss of *Titanic*, two inquiries were set up to attribute blame for the disaster, as well as recommend solutions to ensure such a tragedy never occurred again. The first inquiry was held in the United States while the second was held in Great Britain.

Many of those lost aboard *Titanic* died because the ship, like most ships at the time, did not carry enough lifeboats for all the people on board. Lifeboat carriage aboard ships registered in Great Britain was regulated by the British Board of Trade, which hadn't updated the provision of lifeboat seats since ships were far smaller than *Titanic*. Furthermore, the regulations specified lifeboat carriage based on the vessel's tonnage, rather than its passenger capacity. Calls were immediately made for this archaic practice to be fixed, resulting in lifeboat space for every person aboard. The inquiries further resulted in a long overdue review of safety regulations as well as the establishment of the Safety of Life at Sea (SOLAS) provisions and a marine survey with the task of identifying icebergs.

Shipbuilders also made changes to designs, which were incorporated into *Aquitania*. This new Cunarder was larger than her fleet mates, at

Carmania was built at John Brown & Co., Clydebank, and was fitted with turbine engines. (Ian Boyle/Simplon Postcards)

Lusitania's sleek bow awaiting launch. (Robert Henderson & Doug Cremer Collection)

Lusitania leaving the Clyde after completion. (Robert Henderson & Doug Cremer Collection)

45,647 grt and 901ft long, and was designed to take the travelling public by storm. Her graceful exterior and elegant interiors earned her the nickname 'Ship Beautiful', allowing Cunard to directly compete against the elegant White Star liners.

With safety changes incorporated, *Aquitania* was a far safer ship than those that had come before her. Cunard advertised her safety features, making particular mention of her lifeboat capacity, with seats for all aboard. While pre-*Titanic* ships were often designed to minimise the visual impact of lifeboats, *Aquitania*'s were visible on the deck of the ship, ensuring there were no misconceptions with the general public. The company also emphasised the inclusion of extra watertight compartments that allowed the ship to float with five compartments flooded, either foreword or aft.

Like her running mates, *Aquitania* was completed under the auxiliary armed cruisers agreement, meaning she was available to be called into military service in the event of war, an event that would prove all too soon in arriving.

Lusitania's propellers were each powered by a separate turbine. (Robert Henderson & Doug Cremer Collection)

Lusitania at New York in 1907. (Michael Pocock/Maritime Quest)

Lusitania seen during fit out with the top part of her hull painted white. (Robert Henderson & Doug Cremer Collection)

Mauretania entered service several months after Lusitania. (Ian Boyle/Simplon Postcards)

Q. T. S. S., Mauretania, (THE LARGEST VESSEL IN THE WORLD,) LEAVING THE TYNE.

S.S. MAURETANIA

Above: *Mauretania* makes for an impressive sight when at sea. (Michael Pocock/Maritime Quest)

Mauretania was built at Swan Hunter, Newcastle upon Tyne. (Ian Boyle/Simplon Postcards)

Liner leaving Landing Stage, Liverpool

▶ **DID YOU KNOW?**

Aquitania was one deck taller, 114ft longer and 10ft wider than *Lusitania*.

As an express liner, *Mauretania* was originally based in Liverpool (pictured). In 1919 she inaugurated Cunard's Southampton express service. (Ian Boyle/Simplon Postcards)

Mauretania at Fishguard. (Ian Boyle/Simplon Postcards)

Mauretania at anchor, taking on passengers and supplies. (Ian Boyle/Simplon Postcards)

An artist's impression of *Mauretania* near smaller sailing ships. (Ian Boyle/Simplon Postcards)

This postcard of *Mauretania* was designed to showcase her speed and size. (Ian Boyle/Simplon Postcards)

Mauretania was the world's fastest liner until 1929. (Ian Boyle/Simplon Postcards)

Lusitania captured the transatlantic speed record just months after she entered service in 1907. She later lost the accolade to her sister *Mauretania*. (Robert Henderson & Doug Cremer Collection)

A Cunard postcard of the new *Mauretania*; note the inaccuracy of the bridge design in this artist's impression. (Ian Boyle/Simplon Postcards)

Lusitania towers over the awaiting vehicles in New York. (Robert Henderson & Doug Cremer Collection)

Lusitania's turbine engines utilised steam from coal-fed boilers. As a result emissions were far from clean. (Robert Henderson & Doug Cremer Collection)

There was a lift for first-class passengers aboard *Lusitania* and *Mauretania*. (Robert Henderson & Doug Cremer Collection)

Lusitania's first-class dining room, complete with ornate dome. (Robert Henderson & Doug Cremer Collection)

The veranda café aboard *Mauretania* featured a skylight, living plants and attentive table service. (Robert Henderson & Doug Cremer Collection)

The boat deck of the *Mauretania*, where passengers came to promenade. (Robert Henderson & Doug Cremer Collection)

The first-class dining room aboard *Mauretania* was a magnificent focal point for first class passengers. (Robert Henderson & Doug Cremer Collection)

5

THE FIRST WORLD WAR

We have made a request to the German Government that we shall have a satisfactory assurance as to the Belgium neutrality before midnight tonight. The German reply to our request was unsatisfactory.

British Prime Minister Herbert Henry Asquith, Earl of Oxford, on Britain's declaration of war against Germany

Cunard's new liner, *Aquitania*, entered service for Cunard on 30 May 1914, one day after the Canadian Pacific Steamships' vessel *Empress of Ireland* sank with the loss of 1,012 lives. The disaster marred the festivities planned for *Aquitania*'s maiden voyage with many passengers on board feeling a strong sense of unease during the journey.

In the past decade, Cunard's services had expanded considerably. Not only had the line introduced three express liners, their intermediate services had increased significantly. The line had also increased its ability to carry cargo. This expansion was bolstered by the 1911 purchase of the Thompson Line. The acquisition included the *Albania*, *Ascania* and *Ausonia*. This tonnage was supplemented by the acquisition of the Anchor Line that same year, which added valuable tonnage and routes to the business with the aim of creating a profitable peacetime enterprise.

However, plans for this peacetime service came to a halt less than two months after the *Aquitania*'s maiden voyage. With Britain, France, Russia and their allies at war with Germany and her allies, the First World War

had commenced, and Cunard would face its greatest challenge yet as many of their ships were requisitioned for government service.

Having been built under the auxiliary armed merchant cruisers agreement, *Aquitania* and *Mauretania* were both taken up from service and given refits to make them into armed merchant cruisers. A number of Cunard's earlier express liners, along with their intermediate liners were also called into government service.

Lusitania, though built under the auxiliary armed merchant cruiser agreement, and designed for conversion, never entered into government service. Instead she was kept in merchant service, operating a reduced schedule across the North Atlantic. *Mauretania*, with its almost identical design, did not remain an armed merchant cruiser for long. Her design, though fast, proved unsuitable for the purpose and she was returned to Cunard. The reduced demand for passenger crossings, however, saw her laid up rather than re-entered into service.

The heroic *Carpathia* – seen here in New York – was sunk during the First World War. (Michael Pocock/Maritime Quest)

The war soon spread to the ocean and the North Atlantic became a dangerous place for ships to transit. In an attempt to combat this danger, *Lusitania*'s funnels were painted black to disguise her and she sailed for a time under the then neutral United States flag. Once US President Wilson wrote a letter of protest to the British Admiralty, this practice was stopped. From then on *Lusitania* sailed with no flag at all.

On 7 May 1915, a torpedo fired by German submarine *U-20* struck *Lusitania*. Two explosions ensued and the ship sank off the coast of Ireland with a loss of 1,198 lives. The tragic incident is said to have been a contributing factor in the United States entering into the conflict on the side of the Allies, as there had been American citizens on board who were killed when the ship sank.

After the sinking of the *Lusitania* there was no Cunard ship left in merchant service on the England to New York route. *Mauretania* was intended to be returned to the role but, before this happened, the ship was once again requisitioned by the Admiralty, this time as a troopship, carrying soldiers to the Dardanelles.

In August 1915, *Mauretania* was converted to a hospital ship and placed into service evacuating the wounded from Gallipoli. The ship's interiors were reconfigured once again, this time using the space throughout for hospital beds, wards and operating theatres. The hull was painted white and a series of large red crosses were emblazoned along the vessel to identify her as a hospital ship.

Aquitania made three voyages as a troopship, before she too was converted to a hospital ship. The transition to hospital duties was made possible by the United States' entry into the war. At the time the United States entered the conflict, the majority of the large German liners were

Aquitania's magnificent Palladian Room featured an ornately decorated mural-covered ceiling and a real working fireplace. (Robert Henderson & Doug Cremer collection)

CUNARD LINER "AQUITANIA" LEAVING WAYS—ENTERING WATER

CUNARD LINER "AQUITANIA" LEAVING WAYS—ENTERING WATER

Aquitania was launched in April 1913 at at John Brown in Clydebank. (Ian Boyle/Simplon Postcards)

Aquitania, Cunard's largest ship at the time, takes to the water. (Ian Boyle/Simplon Postcards)

docked in American ports. American authorities seized these ships, including the *Vaterland* and *Imperator*, and placed them into service as troop carriers for America.

Many of Cunard's intermediate liners had also been taken up from trade. This included *Laconia* and *Franconia*, which had entered service in 1912 and 1911 respectively, as well as *Carpathia*, the ship that had rescued the survivors of the *Titanic* disaster. None of these ships would survive the war.

Cunard's 18,150-grt *Franconia* was lost in October 1916, when she was torpedoed off the coast of Malta by *UB-47*. The subsequent sinking resulted in the loss of twelve men, with the survivors collected by *Dover Castle*.

Franconia's sister ship, *Laconia*, was also lost during the war. *Laconia* was operating as an armed merchant cruiser when she was torpedoed by *U-50* off the English coast; again, twelve people died.

Carpathia was lost during 1918 while steaming in a convoy off the coast of England. Three German torpedoes sealed the ship's fate. Five crewmembers were lost, with the survivors being collected by HMS *Snowdrop*.

That same year after being recommissioned as a troop carrier, *Aquitania* collided with the USS *Shaw*, which was assigned to escort the large Cunard liner. The *Shaw*'s helm had jammed, causing the ship to lose manoeuvrability and leaving the stricken vessel in *Aquitania*'s path. With the captain aware that depth charges were stored in the aft end of the *Shaw*, he quickly placed the vessel full astern resulting in *Aquitania* hitting the ship amidships, and though *Shaw* was sliced in two, the captain's actions had averted a greater disaster.

▶ **DID YOU KNOW?**

Campania and *Lucania*'s reciprocating engines were so large that they protruded above the ships' hulls. To protect them, designers created a deck house over the engines.

R. M. S. Aquitania (Cunard Line).
Length 902 ft. Breadth 97 ft.
Depth 92 ft. 6 inches.
Tonnage 47,000. Speed 23 knots.

Left: A postcard claiming to be of Cunard's *Aquitania* inaccurately depicts *Mauretania*. (Ian Boyle/Simplon Postcards)

Below left: Warships and merchant ships alike became targets during the war. (George Frame collection)

Below: The waters around Great Britain became a war zone at the outbreak of the First World War. (George Frame collection)

Elaine MacKay is a name many Cunard cruisers will know; she worked with the line for twenty-three years:

Little did I know, when I went on board *Cunard Princess* in 1980 to do arts and crafts for a one-week cruise, that in less than two years I would give up my teaching career and launch a love affair with an ocean liner that would last just over twenty-three years (but still lingers on today). That one-week cruise hooked me on the joy of cruising. After several such cruises the cruise director, John Butt, said he had recommended me for the *QE2* world cruise as Spanish linguist. I never did that job but joined *QE2* in New York on Columbus Day 1982 as programmer and then social directress, and made more discoveries than Christopher ever thought of. It was the hardest working, most enjoyable job I ever had. I loved the history of Cunard Line and enjoyed sharing it with passengers each voyage. What a majestic lineage for the Great Lady. The ship's beauty, her majestic glide (and sometimes chopping twists in gale-force winds) just added to the thrill. I just loved the transatlantics; after all, that was her heritage and what the Clydebank shipyards built her for and we never knew what Mother Nature would throw our way.

But my favourite part of being on *QE2* was the passengers, celebrity entertainers and crew I met over the years; it truly was a family atmosphere. They all shared in the joy that *QE2* brought. Many pax [passengers] said coming on board was like coming home, and coming back from leave felt like coming home to me. While a big ship for her time, she had a warm, homely atmosphere. I don't really think any other ship has ever had the special connection with the passengers and crew that *QE2* did. World cruise embarkation day was certainly old home week. On any regular embarkation I would always greet our regular return passengers but on a world cruise there were so many more welcome-back greetings and, of course, what other ship could ever dare hang out a 'Welcome Home' banner for returning passengers? They really loved that. I am still in touch with many 'old' passengers and they tell me they have gone on other ships, and they were nice, *but*, they were not the *QE2*.

I remember the 'train parties' in the earlier days, such fun; the Country Fayre; a singer (whom I will not name) mooning the poor guys driving the mules through the Panama Canal; a pax asking Dr Norman Vincent Peale during an interview with me if 'His power of positive thinking had a positive effect on his sex life in later life' – you could have heard a pin drop. I have so many stories and happy memories. I miss my time onboard *QE2* but it is such a joy to still be in touch with so many old shipboard friends.

Cunard's old express liner *Campania*, which had been laid up awaiting scrap prior to the war, was sold to the British Government. She was converted to an aircraft carrier and later earned the distinction of being the first ship to launch aircraft whilst underway.

Caronia, *Carmania* and *Saxonia* were all requisitioned for war service and each of the ships survived; however, tonnage from the Cunard-owned subsidiaries was not so fortunate. The company lost a number of ships from their Anchor Line venture, along with all three ships they had been awarded from the Uranium SS Co. as war reparations in 1916.

▶ **DID YOU KNOW?**

In 1916, Cunard's Anchor Line purchased a controlling share in the Donaldson Line, forming Anchor-Donaldson Line.

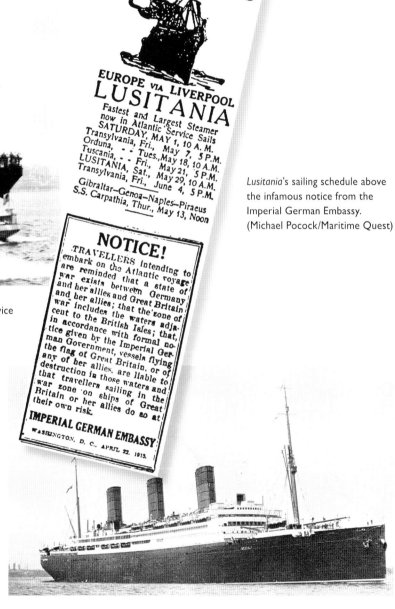

Lusitania's sailing schedule above the infamous notice from the Imperial German Embassy. (Michael Pocock/Maritime Quest)

2015 was the centenary of Lusitania's sinking. In commemoration Cunard held a special service aboard Queen Victoria. (Robert Henderson & Doug Cremer collection)

Cunard's Aquitania served as a hospital ship during the First World War. She was painted white, with red crosses and buff funnels, while in this role. (Ian Boyle/Simplon Postcards)

Imperator (later renamed Berengaria) was Cunard's compensation for the loss of Lusitania. (Robert Henderson & Doug Cremer collection)

6

THE INTERWAR YEARS

Launched the new *Queen Mary* today; pity it rained.

HM Queen Mary journal entry following the
launch of Cunard-White Star's flagship, RMS Queen Mary

Following the cessation of hostilities, a number of the Cunard ships remained in government service. *Aquitania, Mauretania, Caronia, Carmania* and *Saxonia* were all used in the repatriation of American and Canadian troops.

Aquitania and *Mauretania* were able to re-enter passenger service by the end of 1919, after being returned to Cunard and extensively refitted. While it was re-establishing its transatlantic services, Cunard relocated its express hub from Liverpool to Southampton. Southampton offered many benefits, including its proximity to London. *Mauretania* commenced sailing from Southampton on 18 November 1919. Without the *Lusitania*, however, Cunard could not complete their three-ship express service. They resolved this issue when the British Government were awarded a number of German liners as war reparations.

The Hamburg-Amerika liners *Imperator* and *Bismarck* were two of the largest ships of their day. Cunard and White Star Line jointly purchased these ships from the British Government.

Cunard operated *Imperator*, which was one of the more luxurious ships on the market at 900ft long and 52,117 grt. White Star Line was to operate *Bismarck*, which was still under construction at the time of purchase. The third of the large Hamburg-Amerika ships, *Vaterland*, was retained by the United States, becoming the United States Line's flagship *Leviathan*.

Cunard gave *Imperator* a refurbishment and entered her into service as their third express liner in March 1920. She did not remain in service under that name for long, however, and was soon given a major overhaul and renamed as *Berengaria*, becoming the flagship of the Cunard fleet.

With *Berengaria* in service, Cunard were able to re-establish their express services relatively quickly, which meant that they were at the head of the competition again. The German lines had had to surrender their ships to the Allies and were, for now, not a threat.

FASTEST OCEAN SERVICE IN THE WORLD

CUNARD

SOUTHAMPTON, CHERBOURG AND NEW YORK

R.M.S. "MAURETANIA"   R.M.S. "BERENGARIA"   R.M.S. "AQUITANIA"

Above: Cunard's premier liners, *Mauretania*, *Berengaria* and *Aquitania* are seen in this post-war advertising poster. (Ian Boyle/Simplon Postcards)

White Star Line, which returned to British ownership in 1927, was not able to effectively compete with Cunard's express service. Their own three-ship express service was in tatters. They had lost *Titanic* to an iceberg prior to the war and *Britannic* to a mine during the war. As a result the line had only one large express liner, *Olympic*. *Bismarck* took time to complete; however, when she commenced sailing for White Star Line under her new name, *Majestic*, she was one of the greatest ships in service. At 955ft and 56,551 grt, she outstripped even the *Berengaria* and held the title of world's largest ship.

White Star Line also purchased the incomplete Norddeutscher Lloyd liner *Columbus* from His Majesty's Shipping Controller. Renamed *Homeric*, the ship was smaller and slower than their other express liners and was a coal-burning ship, making it time-consuming to refuel between voyages.

In 1922, the *Tyrrhenia* entered service for the Cunard-owned Anchor Line. Built by William Beardmore and Co., the 16,200-grt vessel operated for a short period for Anchor Line before she was refurbished in 1924 with cruising in mind and renamed *Lancastria*. From here on she sailed under the Cunard flag.

Cunard began to build new ships, including their A-class liners, so called because their names all started with the letter A. The fleet consisted of *Antonia*, *Andania*, *Ausonia*, *Aurania*, *Alaunia* and *Ascania*. The first three of the fleet were commissioned in 1922, with *Aurania* in 1924 and the final two in 1925.

The former *Imperator* was refurbished and renamed *Berengaria*. (Ian Boyle/Simplon Postcards)

Berengaria was a welcome addition to the Cunard fleet, taking the title of flagship and becoming a favourite among passengers. (Ian Boyle/Simplon Postcards)

'Jamie Firth served on several of the Cunard *Queens* and recalls his affections for the Cunard Line:

It is a privilege to have a career with Cunard, continuing the legacy that has passed into our care to hand to yet another generation. I have worked with many nationalities, whom over time have become more family than just work colleagues. This has given it a feeling of returning home rather than a workplace each contract. I feel so lucky to have a job that I fully enjoy and that has given me and my family the chance to experience so many countries, meeting so many wonderful passengers along the way. '

Aquitania's design was so exquisite, inside and out, that she was nicknamed the Ship Beautiful throughout her career. (Ian Boyle/Simplon Postcards)

With these intermediate liners, Cunard operated services between Europe and Canada. These routes proved very profitable and increased the awareness of Cunard around the world.

Adding to this, Cunard, in partnership with American Express sent the second *Laconia* on a world cruise in 1922/23. This was to become a Cunard tradition, expanding the Cunard offering and really entering them into the cruising market. Built at Swan Hunter, Newcastle upon Tyne, the *Laconia* was a 19,600-grt vessel. At 601ft long, the ship was of good dimensions to offer a world voyage, providing enough space aboard for the passengers to entertain themselves during the long journey. She was joined by *Franconia*, which, adding to *Scythia* and *Samaria*, completed the series of four intermediate liners designed to undertake cruises.

Cunard further added to its fleet when it commissioned *Carinthia*, which entered service in 1925. At just over 20,000 grt, she was a relatively small ship; however, she was notable for being designed with winter cruising in mind.

On 28 June 1928, the White Star Line laid down a new 1,000ft long liner, to be named *Oceanic*. The design of the new White Star Line ship called for a traditional exterior, which masked her revolutionary machinery. White Star Line, now owned by the Royal Mail Steam Packet Co., had opted for forty diesel engines with the intention of operating the ship at speeds of over 28 knots. However, the cash-poor line was forced to cancel construction in July 1929. The ship was broken up and priority was given to the building of the smaller *Britannic* as well as a sister ship, *Georgic*.

The German lines were not to remain crushed for long. By the time of the stock market crash in 1929, Norddeutscher Lloyd had launched their new express liners the *Bremen* and the *Europa*. *Bremen* and *Europa* eclipsed the Cunard express liners in size, speed and luxury and their profile radically changed the face of ocean liner design. Their modern hull with cruiser stern was paired with a streamlined superstructure and squat funnels, which gave the ships a contemporary appearance. Cunard responded to the threat to their supremacy by laying down a new ship on 1 December 1930 at John Brown Shipyard. To be an 80,000-grt liner, *Hull 534* was intended to win the hearts of the travelling public with its speed and luxury. But Cunard was not the only shipping company laying down new ships.

The newly formed Italia Line (created when Mussolini nationalised Italy's shipping industry) introduced two new liners and entered the transatlantic race. Placing *Rex* and the *Conte di Savoia* into service in 1932, the line was well placed to offer real competition to the British

Aquitania against the New York skyline. (Ian Boyle/Simplon Postcards)

The sheer size of the *Berengaria*, Cunard's flagship is exaggerated in this artist's impression of the ship. (Ian Boyle/Simplon Postcards)

and German lines. While *Rex* was extremely fast and captured the transatlantic speed record, *Conte di Savoia* is renowned as being the first large liner to feature stabilisation technology.

The French Line laid down their 79,280-grt *Normandie* in January 1931. She was to be a rival for Cunard's new ship and also an extremely luxurious and fast ship. *Normandie*'s design was radically different from previous transatlantic liners, with a hydrodynamic hull and turbo-electric engines.

▶ DID YOU KNOW?

Queen Mary's original design had a stern arrangement similar to *Aquitania*, including a separate second-class deck house. This was changed before the ship was built.

By the time *Normandie* was laid down, the impact of the Great Depression was causing great problems for Cunard. Their ageing fleet was crossing the Atlantic emptier than usual due to the prevailing financial conditions. Furthermore, those passengers who were travelling often opted for the newer, faster and more luxurious liners such as *Bremen* or *Europa*.

Cunard attempted to send some of their older tonnage cruising, having moderate success with 'booze cruises' out of America, which was in the midst of Prohibition at the time. But liners such as *Mauretania*, built in 1907 to strict transatlantic specifications, were generally unsuitable as cruise ships and continued to lose money for Cunard.

In December 1931, construction was halted on *Hull 534*. The partially constructed ship was to lie on the slipway, slowly rusting for the next two years. In the meantime the shipyard force was laid off and the community of Clydebank suffered greatly from the lack of employment available.

The French Line, by contrast, was able to continue construction of their ship thanks to government support. The French Government felt it was

Berengaria seen sailing past an English channel fort. (Ian Boyle/Simplon Postcards)

Left: *Berengaria* underway. (Ian Boyle/Simplon Postcards)

Centre: *Berengaria*'s boilers were converted from coal to oil-burning shortly after she entered Cunard service. (Ian Boyle/Simplon Postcards)

Bottom: *Mauretania* was the smallest of Cunard's post-war express trio, however her reputation as world's fastest liner made her a popular ship. (Ian Boyle/Simplon Postcards)

important to show competing powers that France could deliver what was the world's most opulent liner in the midst of a global depression. As such, *Normandie* was launched on 29 October 1932 amid much fanfare.

Unable to complete their new builds, both Cunard and White Star Line each applied to the British Government for financial assistance. The British Government responded to these requests following the receipt of a report by Clydebank MP David Kirkwood. This report explained that the completion of *Hull 534* was in the nation's best interests. The government agreed to provide finance to complete the ship and a running mate, on the proviso that Cunard and White Star Line merged.

Negotiations commenced in 1933 and by 1934 an agreement had been made with Cunard maintaining a controlling interest in the newly formed Cunard-White Star Line. With the merger, twelve White Star Liners, including *Olympic*, *Majestic*, *Homeric*, *Britannic*, *Georgic*, *Laurentic*, *Calgaric*, *Doric*, *Adriatic* and *Albertic* joined the Cunard-White Star fleet. The excess of tonnage meant that Cunard-White Star was forced to retire a number of ships. Most of the vessels that were retired were former White Star Line ships, leaving only *Britannic*, *Georgic* and *Laurentic* by the end of the decade; however, Cunarders including *Mauretania* and *Berengaria* were also scrapped.

The merger of the two lines resulted in funds being provided and construction on *Hull 534* recommenced in April 1934. HM Queen Mary christened the ship *Queen Mary* on 26 September 1934 at her launch and the new ship moved to fitting out, being completed with art deco interiors. The interiors were designed to be comfortable, rather than opulent, whilst still delivering luxury. As a result, she had a very different feel to her French rival, *Normandie*, which had been completed in a more grand and overstated manner. This interior design difference gave *Queen Mary* an edge over *Normandie* with many passengers.

Berengaria's first-class ballroom was one of the finest rooms at sea. (Ian Boyle/Simplon Postcards)

Berengaria's first-class smoking room was completed in an English Tudor style. (Ian Boyle/Simplon Postcards)

Mauretania was smaller than *Aquitania* and *Berengaria* yet remained popular due to her speed. (Ian Boyle/Simplon Postcards)

DID YOU KNOW?

By the 1990s Cunard managed a number of hotels and resorts including:

The Ritz, London
The Dukes, London
The Stafford, London
Hotel Atop the Bellevue, Philadelphia
Watergate, Washington
Hotel La Toc, St Lucia
Paradise Beach, Barbados

Queen Mary set sail on her maiden voyage on 27 May 1936. Queen Mary toured the ship prior to the voyage; writing in her diary of the occasion, 'toured the new *Queen Mary* today. Not as bad as I expected.'

Though fast, *Queen Mary* was not able to capture the Blue Riband on her maiden voyage, which was by now held by the French Line's *Normandie*. Although *Queen Mary* made excellent time during her crossing, she was delayed by fog, making a record-breaking crossing impossible. In August 1936, *Queen Mary* captured the speed record, holding it for a year before losing it to *Normandie* in 1937. A year later she recaptured the record, this time holding it until 1952, with a time of three days, twenty-one hours and forty-eight minutes.

Construction of a running mate for *Queen Mary* commenced on 4 December 1936. Also laid down at the John Brown Shipyard, she was given the yard number *Hull 552*.

Cunard-White Star also commissioned a smaller 35,738-grt liner, which was built at the Cammell Laird yard. Laid down on 24 May 1937, she was launched as *Mauretania* on 28 July 1938 with Lady Bates (wife of Cunard-White Star's chairman) officiating at the ceremony.

Hull 552 was launched on 27 September 1938 by HM Queen Elizabeth, who named the ship for herself. Following this, the newly christened *Queen Elizabeth* was moved to the fitting-out basin.

The new *Mauretania*'s maiden transatlantic crossing commenced on 17 June 1939, just months before the start of the Second World War. *Queen Elizabeth*, on the other hand, was still in Clydebank when hostilities broke out.

▶ **DID YOU KNOW?**

Queen Mary suffered from a significant rolling problem in her early career. It was said that the *Queen Mary* could 'roll the milk out of a cup of tea'.

Mauretania in cruising white, so painted to help cool the hull of the un-air conditioned liner. (Bill Miller)

Above: *Mauretania* and *Olympic* laid up, awaiting scrap. (Michael Pocock/Maritime Quest)

R.M.S. QUEEN MARY.

An artist's impression of *Queen Mary*, with the size of her funnels exaggerated. (Ian Boyle/Simplon Postcards)

Queen Mary's interior was quite different from previous Cunard ships, sporting art deco finishes. This image shows her shopping promenade. (Ian Boyle/Simplon Postcards)

Queen Mary had a children's room, much to the delight of travelling families. (Ian Boyle/Simplon Postcards)

Queen Mary was the pride of the British Merchant Fleet. (Ian Boyle/Simplon Postcards)

Captain Ian McNaught was *QE2*'s last master and is well known among Cunard loyalists:

QE2, what can I say? Being with her was like being married, it had its ups and downs, but you knew she was something special and yes, I loved her to bits.

Of course, she was not everybody's cup of tea. When she first came out, she was radically different from the old Queens, 'Ships have been boring too long' was the slogan. She was very much a ship of the Sixties. Her only competition at the time on the Atlantic was the beautiful *France*, but the British had been brave, and you had *Oriana*, *Canberra* and *QE2* – all fantastic demonstrations of British ingenuity and a huge leap forward from those traditional ships built after the war to replace huge losses.

I can remember as a schoolboy watching the launch on the television, and already wanting to go to sea, something I had inherited from my father. I was fascinated by her; here was something modern, something of its time, something different.

I did not join her until 1987, after some sixteen years at sea. It was immediately after the re-engine project, and more controversy, just like in the beginning. This time it wasn't turbine problems; this time it was Grimm Wheels falling off, and the ship not being ready for passengers. I can remember seeing a picture of Captain Portet in one of the newspapers, with a really disparaging article about the ship and thinking, 'have I done the right thing?'

Once I joined, I never had any doubts. Yes, she had problems, but she just enveloped you and drew you in and you became part of something greater than yourself.

Transatlantic crossings were fantastic, this four-day dash across the ocean at 29 knots. It was a voyage with real purpose, no matter what the weather, and the ship just took on this four-day routine to entertain the passengers: captain's receptions, cabin parties, church service on Sunday mornings, black-tie dinners, afternoon tea served by waiters with white gloves, and lectures from some of the biggest names around at the time. The ship did not need the outside world for those four days, it was like magic, and before you knew it, you were berthing in Pier 90, Manhattan.

Totally different was the world cruise. After the Christmas Caribbean cruise, the ship would transform itself into a totally different atmosphere, with passengers on board until the end of April for this leisurely circumnavigation of the world. Everybody knew everybody, passengers would book the same cabin year after year, and the whole ship just relaxed and enjoyed itself. How could you not? As well as all the small places, you had three days in Hong Kong, three days in Sydney, and fantastic tours for passengers: safaris in Kenya, Agra in India, the Great Wall of China, just to name a few.

But it was not all about passengers. The heart and soul of the ship was the ship's company, and it was these 1,020 people who made her what she was; it was them who gave the ship her character. To some passengers I don't think it mattered where the ship was, they had come to enjoy the ship and the crew. We had a very close relationship with our passengers, and I think some of the more modern, larger tonnage must miss out on the contact between passengers and crew. There were still many crew members who, when we took her to Dubai in 2008, had been there since the maiden voyage, virtually forty years' service in one ship. I can remember one restaurant manager who only had three ships in his discharge book, *Queen Mary*, *Queen Elizabeth* and *QE2*. The loyalty to *QE2* was enormous, and you cannot buy that, or pretend … it was real and tangible – and it did not matter what your job was in the ship, you were part of something special.

There are many special memories for me. I suppose the first time you take command is a unique day; all of a sudden it is all yours and everybody is looking at you to provide order and direction. This is what you have worked for all your life, to be in command of the most famous ship in the world, and sailing out of Southampton that day, having cleared Nab Tower and set speed for New York, to come down from the bridge into the captain's quarters for your supper just made me feel very humble, but proud, and, to be honest, a little nervous. It was the beginning of a great adventure.

In 2007, we had a cruise around the UK to celebrate her fortieth anniversary since launching on the Clyde, and I had the great thrill of taking her to River Tyne, my home port. As we came up from Southampton the weather just got worse and worse, until we arrived off the Tyne in black skies, driving rain and strong winds. 'Sorry we are not going in,' I said. I could see that the locals had turned out in their thousands, and it was a tidal river, so we only had a short window. Well, we went round three times off the entrance until, on the fourth time round, you could see blue sky up river and the evening sun appearing and the wind beginning to drop, so in we went. I shall never forget that welcome, thousands had waited so patiently in the wind and the rain to see her come in, and to be able to bring my ship home made me feel quite humble and proud.

We also had the honour of entertaining HM the Queen on board in June of 2008. She toured the ship and met crew members and passengers, and enjoyed lunch in the Caronia Restaurant, and for me to be the host on behalf of the ship's company was a great honour. It became very obvious as we toured the ship that Her Majesty has a huge affection and understanding for ships. One of the highlights was when we went on to the bridge wing, and QM2 was in further up river, and she was asked if she would blow our ship's whistle in return to the salute from QM2, which she enjoyed doing. But what really made my day was, as she was looking at QM2, her comments about the design of modern ships – and what she said will remain private between me and Her Majesty!

The last Royal visit was by HRH the Duke of Edinburgh on 11 November 2008, the day of the final call in Southampton before we sailed to Dubai. And what a day that was! The duke, a sailor himself of course, enjoyed his visit and lunched in the Princess Grill. Very soon it was time for departure, and the city of Southampton did us proud: fantastic fireworks, music, crowds on the shore all the way down river and hundreds of small boats around us – I don't think there was anybody who did not shed a tear that evening. It was a sad but glorious celebration of the ship and her long relationship with the port of Southampton.

Only days later we arrived in Dubai on 26 November, with a wonderful arrival salute from HMS Lancaster, who manned the side to salute QE2, the only time that has ever been done for a merchant ship. The next day, passengers disembarked and we handed the ship over to her new owners at a formal ceremony on the bridge where the Cunard House Flag, our paying off pennant and Red Ensign were lowered for the last time, and the flags of Dubai and Nakheel, the new owners, were raised.

I have to say, for me, and the other officers on the bridge wing, the staff captain, the chief engineer and the hotel manager, that was one of the most painful and heart-breaking moments of our lives. It really brought home that QE2 was gone, and no matter what they did to her thereafter, she would not be the QE2 we had known and loved all those years.

The modern ships have changed now to satisfy a new market and I can honestly say that we will never see the likes of her again. She will be sadly missed by all who sailed in her, both passengers and crew.

Queen Mary sailing on the North Atlantic Ocean. (Ian Boyle/Simplon Postcards)

Queen Mary seen here under the assistance of tugs. (Ian Boyle/Simplon Postcards)

Queen Mary held the speed record until 1952. (Ian Boyle/Simplon Postcards)

7

THE SECOND WORLD WAR

Built for the arts of peace and to link the Old World with the New, the Queens challenged the fury of Hitlerism in the Battle of the Atlantic. Without their aid the day of final victory must unquestionably have been postponed.

Sir Winston Churchill, 1946

The Second World War was to plunge Cunard-White Star back into armed conflict, with their ships once again at risk. At the outbreak of war, *Queen Mary* was safe in New York harbour, having just completed her 143rd crossing.

The decision was made in early 1940 that *Queen Elizabeth* had to leave Clydebank. In preparation for the voyage, the ship was painted all over in grey and given a degaussing coil to help her avoid damage from mines. Leaving the Clyde was a delicate process that required certain tidal conditions. As such, *Queen Elizabeth* had to wait until 26 February 1940 to make the journey to the Tail o' the Bank. The following day, the ship was handed over to her owners, despite not yet having had her sea trials.

It was widely believed that *Queen Elizabeth* would be sent to Southampton, where a fitting-out basin had been prepared for her. Winston Churchill, however, secretly ordered the ship to leave British waters, as she was a priority target for the Luftwaffe. The crew was not given a destination, but required to sign articles for an international voyage. Those unwilling to sign were detained until after the ship's sailing.

Sealed orders were sent to the ship, arriving on 2 March 1940, which were only to be opened once the ship was at sea. She sailed that day at 7.30 a.m., heading towards Northern Ireland. At 11 p.m. that same day Captain Townley opened the orders, discovering that his destination was New York.

The ship made a dash across the North Atlantic Ocean at 27.5 knots, her launching gear still attached, and arrived at her destination six days later. In New York she was berthed beside *Mauretania* and *Queen Mary*, as well as the French liner *Normandie*.

The ships were not to sit idle for long. Their size meant that they were ideal for trooping duties and as a result the British Admiralty soon requisitioned the Cunard-White Star ships for use in the war effort. *Mauretania* was sent to Sydney for conversion, departing New York on 20 March 1940. *Queen Mary* departed the following day for the same destination, via a different route.

One of the most terrible wartime losses was that of Cunard-White Star's *Lancastria*, which was sunk on 17 June 1940, off the coast of St Nazaire, whilst taking part in the evacuation of Western France. The loss of life was so great that the British Government banned announcement of the disaster, with the news taking five weeks to reach the public. There is no accurate record of how many people were aboard the ship when it sunk, though the number is estimated to be more than 6,000. Only 2,477 people were rescued from the wreck.

Queen Elizabeth sailed from New York for Singapore on 13 November 1940, to be converted to the world's largest troopship. Following her conversion, she joined *Mauretania*, *Aquitania* and *Queen Mary* in transporting Australian and New Zealand soldiers to the war zone.

The last of the White Star liners, *Britannic* and *Georgic*, were also called into service. *Britannic* had a very successful wartime career, and carried approximately 180,000 troops during the conflict.

Georgic did not enjoy the same luck. The Luftwaffe bombed her on 14 July 1941, whilst anchored at Port Tewfik, Suez. Her captain ordered her driven on to a reef so as not to block the harbour and she burned out. She was later refloated and sent to Harland & Wolff for an extensive refit and returned to military service, minus one funnel and with only a foremast.

▶ **DID YOU KNOW?**

When *Queen Elizabeth* made her first transatlantic crossing, she still had her launching gear attached under the waterline.

After America entered the war, *Queen Elizabeth* and *Queen Mary* were given further refits to allow them to carry even more soldiers. They then commenced troop transporting duties, carrying American servicemen to Europe.

The events around the sinking of Cunard-White Star's *Laconia* were to forever change the operations of the German U-boat fleet. *Laconia* was torpedoed and sunk on 12 September 1942. She was carrying civilians and Italian prisoners of war, in addition to soldiers. Following the sinking, the U-boat captain and his crew commenced rescue operations, then proceeded to rendezvous with Vichy French ships, under the Red Cross banner, to transfer survivors.

Cunard's second *Mauretania* didn't sail for long in passenger service before the Second World War broke out. (Ian Boyle/Simplon Postcards)

Three Cunarders in wartime convoy – *Queen Mary*, *Queen Elizabeth* and *Mauretania*. (Robert Henderson & Doug Cremer collection)

At the outbreak of the Second World War, the ocean became a battlefield once again and ships from all flags were destroyed. Cunard's fleet was a highly prized target for the Luftwaffe. (George Frame collection)

Whilst underway, the U-boat was bombed by an American bomber. From this time on, the U-boat captains abandoned the practice of attempting to rescue civilian survivors under the 'Laconia Order'. This set the precedent for unrestricted submarine warfare, which devastated Allied shipping.

Queen Mary was involved in the sinking of a British naval vessel in a tragic accident on 2 October 1942. The Queens were very effective troopships; carrying over 15,000 soldiers per voyage, but this also made them a very high priority target for unfriendly forces. As a result, both Queen Mary and Queen Elizabeth were under orders to steam at high speeds when crossing the Atlantic, and not to stop for any reason.

Queen Mary and Queen Elizabeth were both assigned naval escorts in an attempt to protect them, but the two ships were so fast that they often outstripped their escorts. On the day of the incident, Queen Mary's escort was the light cruiser, HMS Curacao.

In an accidental manoeuvre, Curacao cut across Queen Mary's path on their approach to Scotland. Due to the speed at which she was travelling, there was no time for Queen Mary to avoid the collision and she ploughed into the naval vessel, slicing the smaller ship in half. The captain and officers were unable to stop to attempt to rescue survivors, and instead *Queen Mary* continued on, with four other destroyer escorts pulling the survivors from the ocean.

In January 1945, the Cunard-White Star liner *Franconia* was selected as the base for the British delegation at the Yalta Conference. The purpose of this historic event, which took place between 4 February and 11 February, was to facilitate a meeting between Churchill, Roosevelt and Stalin, at which the three leaders discussed the post-war reorganisation of Europe.

With the 8 May 1945 unconditional surrender of Germany, the war in Europe was at an end. Cunard-White Star Line, as well as all other transatlantic shipping operators, was now faced with the mammoth task of repatriation and rebuilding.

The two largest troop carriers the world has ever seen, *Queen Mary* and *Queen Elizabeth*, had remained in military service as troopships for the duration of the war. At the end of the conflict they were hailed as national heroes. Their ability to carry such high numbers of troops on each crossing led to Winston Churchill remarking that they had shortened the length of the war by at least a year.

Escorts were sent to protect the troop ships; the Cunard Queens often outpaced the slower naval vessels. (George Frame collection)

Christopher Rynd recently retired from a lifetime at sea. He was master of all four modern Queens – *QE2*, *QM2*, *Queen Victoria* and *Queen Elizabeth* – and held the title of Commodore of Cunard Line. He reflects on taking *Queen Mary 2* into Sydney for the first time, during her 2007 World Cruise:

Approaching Sydney heads in early twilight, it was a calm clear morning, and filling the approaches could only be seen hundreds of lights, those of the fleet of small vessels out to welcome us, so many that it seemed that there was no channel through. *Queen Mary 2*'s arrival was timed to be in the centre of the harbour with the iconic Harbour Bridge and Opera House in view at the moment of sunrise and all provided a glorious sight for those on board and viewing her. We berthed at the Garden Island by special arrangement with the Royal Australian Navy. That afternoon the famous *Queen Elizabeth 2* arrived to rendezvous with us and the city came to a stop such were the spectator crowds. When *Queen Mary 2* sailed that evening there were fireworks and an exchange of whistle signals and in the air a carnival atmosphere the knowledge that we were all part of a grand and historic event.

Left: Cunard-White Star's *Georgic* was bombed by the Luftwaffe. She burnt out and sunk but was later refloated and repaired. (George Frame collection)

Below: Cunard's *Queen Mary* as a troopship. This image was taken in Sydney Harbour. (Robert Henderson & Doug Cremer collection)

Queen Elizabeth commenced her career as a troop ship. (Michael Pocock/Maritime Quest)

Mauretania was used for trooping duties. She is seen here en route to the Gulf of Suez. (George Frame collection)

Lancastria was sunk in June 1940, resulting in a shocking loss of life. (Ian Boyle/ Simplon Postcards)

Artist Robert Lloyd shares his recollections of a Royal unveiling:

Early in 2008, it was announced the famous ocean liner *Queen Elizabeth 2* would be retired. To mark her retirement, I was commissioned by Cunard to produce a painting to celebrate her time in service and was to depict her final arrival in Southampton. The painting was to be titled 'Coming Home' and was to be large at 6x4ft.

As the painting progressed, I was told that it was going to be unveiled at a special event onboard in the Queens Room and that the person to unveil it was to be Her Majesty The Queen!

As the event drew closer, I started to receive more details and was told that I would meet the Queen and would be asked questions, not only about myself but also about the painting. I then received letters of instruction from the palace, how to address Her Majesty, things to say and not to say. I had to provide a brief resume about myself and my work so she would already know something about me.

The painting itself was complete and featured the ship sailing down Southampton Water surrounded by small craft. On my paintings I always try to add some personal touches, in this case many of the small craft bore names of my family: my children Emilia and Lily and my wife Vicky. The final touch was to add in a small cartoon monkey, hidden somewhere until someone with very sharp eyes spots it. You might call it a 'trademark' and it features in all my paintings, but I never tell anyone where it is. All this was written in the Queen's briefing.

On the day, I waited nervously in line as the Queen approached. She was introduced to crew members, dignitaries and company executives. I was told she would unveil the painting, then I would be introduced and a brief conversation then she would move on.

Finally, she approached. I was introduced by Carol Marlow who at the time was President of Cunard. The Queen said how much she liked the painting, she asked me to point out the boats with the family names, asked how long it took to complete, what was my inspiration – all of the usual and expected questions. Then she gave me a small smile and asked where she would find the monkey. Standing behind her Carol Marlow was mouthing, 'Tell her, tell her', but I said, 'I am very sorry, Ma'am, I am afraid I cannot do that.' There was a moment of complete silence and I thought 'oh no I've blown it'. She looked at me closely and, with a little twinkle in her eye, said 'you know, in years gone by I could have sent you to "the Tower", I will endeavour to get someone to find it for me,' and again she smiled.

It was one of those moments I will never forget.

A couple of weeks later I received a letter from the palace saying the Queen was pleased to meet me and was most impressed by the painting. The letter stated that the Queen enjoyed completing jigsaw puzzles with the family over Christmas and therefore would it be possible to produce one of the painting? Luckily, I was acquainted with a company who produced high quality jigsaw puzzles who immediately agreed to produce a one-off, as they said the kudos made it worthwhile. Pushing my luck, I asked if they would produce just one more for me, happily they agreed.

In November 2008 one almost unique 5,000-piece jigsaw puzzle was delivered to the palace, resplendent in an embossed leather box with a beautifully engraved plate marking the occasion on the front. The puzzle itself was held in a silk bag inside the box. A second one exactly the same arrived at my door just a few days later. Of course, I still have it.

In January I received a letter from the palace saying how much the Queen and her family had enjoyed completing the puzzle and thank you. At the base of the letter was a small note saying 'and Her Majesty would just like you to know she finally found the monkey!'

Queen Mary painted grey as a troop vessel. She was refitted to carry upwards of 10,000 troops on each voyage. (Robert Henderson & Doug Cremer collection)

In this wartime view, *Queen Elizabeth* is carrying over 10,000 troops. Such a sight was commonplace during the Second World War and resulted in a strict regime aboard to provide maximum comfort and ensure the ship's stability. (Robert Henderson & Doug Cremer collection)

Queen Elizabeth in Sydney harbour.
(Robert Henderson & Doug
Cremer collection)

▶ **DID YOU KNOW?**

All four of Cunard's large express liners – *Queen Elizabeth*, *Queen Mary*, *Mauretania* and *Aquitania* – survived service in the Second World War.

Queen Mary's troops as the ship prepares to depart. (Robert Henderson & Doug Cremer collection)

S.S. QUEEN MARY & QUEEN ELIZABETH FROM THE AIR.

Above right: *Queen Mary* in her wartime livery, but with her funnel colours restored. (Ian Boyle/Simplon Postcards)

Above: *Queen Mary* – undertaking warbride repatriation – passes her sister, *Queen Elizabeth*, at the end of their military service. (Ian Boyle/Simplon Postcards)

The two Queens at the end of their wartime service. *Queen Elizabeth* (left) painted in civilian colours while *Queen Mary* (right) retains her wartime grey. (Ian Boyle/Simplon Postcards)

8

POST-WAR RECOVERY

Getting there is half the fun.

Cunard advertising slogan from the 1950s

The Allied victory in Europe meant that Cunard-White Star's requisitioned tonnage was no longer required for the dangerous and highly demanding trooping operation. However, Cunard-White Star did not immediately regain use of their ships.

Cunard-White Star's four largest liners, *Queen Mary*, *Queen Elizabeth*, *Mauretania* and *Aquitania*, were used for several months to repatriate American and Canadian soldiers and their brides. The additional service meant that it took some time before Cunard-White Star was in a position to resume their Atlantic express service.

Queen Elizabeth was the first to be released from government service. She was returned to Clydebank where she was fitted out for the first time as a passenger ship and finally received and passed her builders' sea trials. *Queen Mary* was released from service in September 1946. She was given an extensive refit where she was reconditioned to her pre-war glory.

With their two express liners in commercial service Cunard-White Star was able to finally commence the world's first two-ship weekly transatlantic service. *Queen Mary* and *Queen Elizabeth* proved very popular with the travelling public. The ships were fast and reliable and the Cunard-White Star service was, for a time, the quickest and most luxurious way to travel the North Atlantic.

Once again the other European lines had been decimated by the war, leaving little competition for Cunard-White Star on the express service. Cunard-White Star was also running other services with their restored intermediate liners, and ex-express liners.

Aquitania had once again survived the war and re-entered Cunard-White Star service in 1946, being then chartered by the Canadian Government to transport war brides and their children to Canada. She remained in this role until 1949, when she was laid up as she was too costly to refit to new safety standards.

Mauretania, which had entered service just prior to the outbreak of the Second World War, was able to resume her Atlantic service in 1947, after extensive refurbishment at her builders, Cammell Laird & Co.

The last of the White Star liners, *Britannic* and *Georgic*, returned to passenger services, with *Britannic*'s first peacetime passenger voyage occurring in 1948. *Georgic*'s wartime foundering meant that she was never quite the same again, with the ship plagued by heavy vibrations from the extensive and hasty rebuilding effort. She was managed and operated by Cunard-White Star, running services for the Ministry of Transport.

While *Britannic* was placed on the prestigious Liverpool to New York route, *Georgic* was used for the immigrant trade between the UK and Australia and New Zealand, under the assisted passage scheme. *Georgic* resumed transatlantic services in 1950 and was laid up in 1954, having been used as a troopship in the Korean War. Following this, she briefly re-entered service on the Australian passage before being laid up again.

Cunard was soon to supplement their fleet with new post-war tonnage. *Parthia* and *Media* entered service for Cunard in 1947. These ships were designed and built as combination cargo and passenger ships. Each ship had room for 250 first-class passengers, in addition to their cargo-carrying capacity. The privacy afforded by having such a small passenger complement meant that they became quite popular with travelling celebrities, who often found it difficult to keep up appearances on larger liners such as the Queens.

In 1947, the company became known as Cunard Line once again, after Cunard bought out White Star Line's interest in the organisation. Despite the name change, the White Star pennant continued to be flown from the aft mast aboard the two remaining White Star ships, *Britannic* and *Georgic*, until each ship's retirement. Furthermore, both liners retained their White Star livery and buff-coloured funnels.

On 30 October 1947, Cunard's Green Goddess, *Caronia*, was launched in a ceremony presided over by HRH Princess Elizabeth. This was the princess' last official engagement before her marriage to Prince Philip. A dual-purpose ship, *Caronia* earned her nickname due to being painted in four shades of green, rather than the traditional Cunard matt black hull with white superstructure. This colour scheme was purposely chosen to signify that this ship was designed for cruising and gave her an instantly recognisable and unique identity.

To satisfy the dual-purpose design, *Caronia* maintained the traditional ocean liner traits of speed, strength and stability. However, *Caronia* was completed with several features making her suitable for cruising. She had large picture windows, affording excellent views of cruising destinations, while a large outdoor swimming pool and lido area allowed passengers to enjoy the outdoors while the ship was cruising in the tropics.

Queen Elizabeth held the record as the world's largest passenger ship until 1996 when she was finally eclipsed by *Carnival Destiny*. (Ian Boyle/Simplon Postcards)

Queen Mary makes way from New York Harbour in her peacetime livery. (Ian Boyle/Simplon Postcards)

With her twin funnels and clutter-free decks, *Queen Elizabeth* appeared visually modern when compared to *Queen Mary*. (Ian Boyle/Simplon Postcards)

Cunard's new flagship and the world's largest liner, *Queen Elizabeth*. (Ian Boyle/Simplon Postcards)

The *Queen Mary* at sea. (Ian Boyle/Simplon Postcards)

Caronia entered service in January 1949, with a maiden voyage across the Atlantic. After several more Atlantic crossings, she made her first cruise voyage to the Caribbean that same year and carved out a reputation of excellence, attracting a loyal following for the remainder of her career.

Aside from the primary transatlantic liners, other liners, such as the 1923 built *Franconia* and her sisters *Scythia* and *Samaria*, were returned to passenger service. Having been built as replacement tonnage for ships lost during the First World War, these three ships survived the Second World War and, following repatriation duties, were utilised by Cunard on supplementary transatlantic voyages throughout the 1950s until their retirement.

In 1951, Cunard acquired further cargo tonnage when they purchased the 1948-built *Silverplane* and *Silverbriar* from the Silver Line. Renamed *Alsatia* and *Andria*, the combination liners were converted into dedicated freighters, remaining in Cunard service until 1963.

In 1952, *Queen Mary* lost her title as holder of the transatlantic speed records when the United States Lines introduced their new flagship, SS *United States*. The American Government wanted a large liner that

Queen Elizabeth as seen from the air. Note the wash from the propellers as the mighty liner berths. (Ian Boyle/Simplon Postcards)

'

Caroline Scallan was the head of Cunard's enrichment programme and booked many famous people to speak aboard Cunard's fleet:

Cunard is one of the most recognisable brands. Working at Cunard was a privilege. I always felt like I was part of something really special – watching historic moments from ship launches, royal visits and guests enjoying the unique White Star Service offered aboard Cunard's ships.

'

could be used as a troop ship, should the need arise, and, as a result, built an extremely fast ship. Cunard considered refurbishing *Queen Elizabeth* in order to recapture the record; however, *United States'* average speed of 34 knots was unbeatable.

In 1953, *Media* received a refit, which included the introduction of fin stabilisers aboard. This refit was so successful that the technology was later rolled out to other Cunard liners.

Alsatia and *Andria* were soon joined by new-build cargo vessels, including *Pavia* and *Phrygia*. Built in Glasgow by William Hamilton & Co., they entered service for Cunard in 1953 and 1955 respectively. These 3,500-grt vessels operated cargo services for Cunard until they were sold in 1965.

In 1954, the *Saxonia*-class liners were introduced on to the Canadian route. Four near-identical sisters, each ship grossed approximately 21,600 grt. The fleet, comprising *Saxonia*, *Ivernia*, *Carinthia* and *Sylvania*, settled into a schedule of crossings at a time when pressurized piston-driven airliners were gaining popularity.

But by the time the *Saxonia*-class liners entered service, the transatlantic landscape was starting to shift. A revolution in commercial aircraft design was about to change Cunard forever.

Cunard's *Queen Elizabeth* being handled by tugboats. (Ian Boyle/Simplon Postcards)

Unlike *Queen Mary*, *Queen Elizabeth* had clutter-free top decks as her ventilation was clustered under her twin funnels. (Ian Boyle/Simplon Postcards)

Queen Elizabeth required tug assistance to manouvre in close quarters. (Robert Henderson & Doug Cremer collection)

The Cunard Line flagship arrives in Cunard's British hub at Southampton. (Ian Boyle/ Simplon Postcards)

Passers-by catch a glimpse of *Queen Mary*. (Ian Boyle/Simplon Postcards)

Queen Elizabeth docked in Southampton at the end of another crossing. (Ian Boyle/ Simplon Postcards)

Queen Elizabeth passes the skyscrapers of lower Manhattan. (Ian Boyle/ Simplon Postcards)

Queen Elizabeth on a perfect ocean. (Ian Boyle/Simplon Postcards)

Queen Elizabeth picking up speed as she heads out to sea. (Ian Boyle/Simplon Postcards)

Queen Mary departs on a transatlantic voyage. (Ian Boyle/Simplon Postcards)

Queen Mary had three funnels that were used to ventilate her twenty-four boilers. (Ian Boyle/Simplon Postcards)

Mauretania's profile shared many features with *Queen Elizabeth*. (Ian Boyle/ Simplon Postcards)

Mauretania was smaller than the Queens yet still a popular ship. (Ian Boyle/Simplon Postcards)

Mauretania's (pictured) intended sister was redesigned into the *Caronia*. (Ian Boyle/ Simplon Postcards)

Cunard opted to paint *Caronia* in a green livery that led to her nickname of the Green Goddess. (Ian Boyle/Simplon Postcards)

Caronia was built with cruising in mind. (Ian Boyle/Simplon Postcards)

Caronia was unique in her design, with the widest funnel at sea and a single mast. (Ian Boyle/Simplon Postcards)

Caronia was painted in four shades of green, giving her a distinctive appearance. (Ian Boyle/Simplon Postcards)

Caronia on a cruise with flags flying and anchor dropped. (Ian Boyle/Simplon Postcards)

Her cruising role took *Caronia* to exotic destinations. (Ian Boyle/Simplon Postcards)

As a smaller combination liner, *Media*'s quiet and intimate onboard atmosphere made her popular with celebrities. (Ian Boyle/Simplon Postcards)

Parthia was small and private, enticing to stars of screen and stage. (Ian Boyle/ Simplon Postcards)

An artist's impression of the 1954 *Saxonia*. (Ian Boyle/Simplon Postcards)

▶ **DID YOU KNOW?** ....

The original Queens used nearly 1,000 tons of fuel per day on the transatlantic run.

Saxonia was the class leader for the *Saxonia* sisters. (Ian Boyle/Simplon Postcards)

Saxonia en route to Canada. This class of ship featured a dome-topped funnel. (Ian Boyle/Simplon Postcards)

When times got tough, Cunard sent their ships cruising Here *Franconia* can be seen in her post-cruising guise. (Ian Boyle/Simplon Postcards)

Carmania (ex-*Saxonia*) in *Caronia*-inspired green livery. (Ian Boyle/Simplon Postcards)

▶ DID YOU KNOW?

While the *Saxonia*-class liners had luxurious first-class accommodation, their tourist class was well behind the times. The accommodation was small and most cabins did not have private bathrooms.

Carmania and *Franconia* were treated to significant refurbishments, including a paint scheme similar to *Caronia*'s for their cruising role. (Ian Boyle/Simplon Postcards)

Queen Mary at the iconic, 1950s art deco Ocean Terminal, Southampton. (Ian Boyle/Simplon Postcards)

Queen Elizabeth made many transatlantic crossings during her career. (Ian Boyle/Simplon Postcards)

Queen Elizabeth was designed in an era before bow and stern thrusters were commonplace. As a result she required tug assistance when docking at Southampton. (Ian Boyle/Simplon Postcards)

9

THE AGE OF THE JET

Flying is a fad.

An unnamed Cunard director

In 1957, even before commercial jet services became commonplace, for the first time more passengers crossed the Atlantic by air than by ocean liner.

Cunard's transatlantic passenger numbers had been reducing over the previous years, since the introduction of regular airliner services on the Lockheed Constellation and Douglas DC-6 and -7, while the British-built Comet 4 offered the first transatlantic jet services; albeit on a relatively small scale. With the introduction of Boeing's immensely popular 707, the era of the transatlantic liner was coming to an end. Passengers flocked to the airlines and the diminished passenger numbers meant that many of Cunard's ships were no longer suitable for their current roles.

Scythia was scrapped in 1958, having become the longest-serving Cunarder to that date; *Georgic* was scrapped in 1956, and *Britannic* in 1960, putting an end to the last remnants of the White Star Line. In 1961, both *Media* and *Parthia* left the Cunard fleet, sold to other shipping companies.

Cunard had been planning a new ship, codenamed *Q3*, which was to be an updated version of their current Queens. However, on 19 October 1961, these plans were abandoned. Cunard could not justify building another ship of similar dimensions when their current ships were losing profitability. Instead they began to consider new options.

Mauretania was converted for cruising in 1962, undergoing an extensive refurbishment and being repainted in varying shades of green, to match *Caronia*. *Ivernia* and *Saxonia* were also given cruising refits, with both ships having their aft decks altered to add a swimming pool and lido area. Following their refits they were renamed *Franconia* and *Carmania*.

Also in 1962, Cunard entered into a joint venture agreement with the British Overseas Airways Corporation to form BOAC-Cunard. This subsidiary airline operated flights from the UK to North America and the tropics.

In 1965, *Queen Elizabeth* was given a refit, with air conditioning installed and her aft decks modified to include a lido deck and swimming pool, much like the refits given to other ships. It was hoped that this refit would allow *Queen Elizabeth* to perform a dual-purpose role – cruising and transatlantic line voyages. Unfortunately, *Queen Elizabeth* proved too large for such a purpose.

Queen Mary was also sent cruising in the quieter months, but without the additional changes that *Queen Elizabeth* had been given she proved even less successful as a cruise ship. Both *Queen Mary* and *Queen Elizabeth* were too large to transit the Panama Canal, seriously restricting their ability to visit different ports. They both also had deep draughts, which meant that they were unable to enter the shallower ports of the Caribbean and Mediterranean, further restricting their cruising capabilities.

On 30 December 1964, it had been announced that John Brown & Co. of Clydebank, Scotland had won the tender to build Cunard's latest ocean liner. Codenamed *Q4*, this ship was to be smaller than the *Queen Mary* and *Queen Elizabeth*. She was to be built as a dual-purpose liner, with dimensions small enough to enable her to transit the Panama Canal, and a draught shallow enough to allow her to enter most cruising ports. Her keel was laid down on 5 July 1965. The building of this new ship was partially financed by the British Government on the understanding that the ship be built in the UK. The rest of the finance came from mortgaging eleven of Cunard's existing ships.

In November 1965, *Mauretania* was retired. She had been making losses and Cunard could no longer maintain her in her role. She was sold for scrap, departing Southampton on 20 November 1965.

Attempts were made to transform other Cunard ships into part-time cruise ships. *Sylvania* was given a refurbishment for cruising in 1965, though this was not as extensive as the refits her sister ships had received years before. As a result, she was less successful in her new role than they. The fourth of the *Saxonia* sisters, *Carinthia*, was given a partial cruising refit later that decade but again, as it was not complete the refit did not greatly extend the ship's life with Cunard.

BOAC bought out Cunard's share of the BOAC-Cunard joint venture in 1966. This freed up more capital for Cunard, though it was not enough to halt the requirement to sell tonnage to fund their new build. On 8 May 1967, the captains of *Queen Mary* and *Queen Elizabeth* learned the fate of their ships whilst at sea. Both ships were to become floating hotels in America.

Mauretania was sent cruising before she was sold for scrap. (Ian Boyle/Simplon Postcards)

Queen Mary is farewelled from Southampton for the final time. (Ian Boyle/Simplon Postcards)

On 20 September 1967, Q4 was officially launched. HM Queen Elizabeth II presided over the ceremony, naming the ship *Queen Elizabeth the Second*. As there was already a Royal Naval vessel with the name *Queen Elizabeth II*, Cunard applied to Buckingham Palace, receiving permission to name their new vessel *Queen Elizabeth 2*, using the number 2, rather than the Roman numeral, to distinguish the two ships.

Queen Mary's departure from the Cunard fleet happened later that year. She sailed from Southampton for the final time on 31 October, bound for California. The voyage was her longest ever peacetime voyage, with the ship going via Cape Horn.

With fitting out and engine troubles, *Queen Elizabeth 2* took almost a further two years before she entered service. During that time, more ships left the Cunard fleet. In 1968, *Caronia* was withdrawn from service and sold to Star Shipping. *Carinthia* and *Sylvania* were both sold to the Sitmar Line, where they were given full cruising refits and renamed *Fairsea* and *Fairwind*. They remained in cruising roles under various operators until 2005 and 2004 respectively.

Queen Elizabeth also departed the Cunard fleet that year. She was renamed *Elizabeth* and plans were created for her to become a floating hotel in Fort Lauderdale, in a joint venture between Cunard and a group

▶ **DID YOU KNOW?**

Seawise University (the former *Queen Elizabeth*) never opened as a university. Prior to the completion of her conversion, several fires broke out aboard and she burnt out and sank in Hong Kong harbour.

Queen Elizabeth briefly opened as an attraction at Fort Lauderdale. (Ian Boyle/Simplon Postcards)

QE2's bulbous bow being attached. (Cunard/Michael Gallagher)

The great bow of Number 736, awaiting launch. (Cunard/ Michael Gallagher)

Launched and named *Queen Elizabeth 2*, she is seen here at the fitting-out basin. (Cunard/Michael Gallagher)

QE2's mast was very different in style to her forbears. This gave the ship a more modern, racy appearance. (Cunard/Michael Gallagher)

QE2's mast being attached atop the bridge. (Cunard/Michael Gallagher)

Cunard's new flagship, *Queen Elizabeth 2*. (Cunard/Michael Gallagher)

The Grill Room aboard *QE2* had sculptures that dominated the décor. (Cunard/Michael Gallagher)

QE2 on sea trials. (Cunard/Michael Gallagher)

of Philadelphia business owners. Never officially converted, the ship lingered in Fort Lauderdale, opening briefly as a hotel in her original format. The lack of funds meant the plans fell through fairly quickly. She was sold in 1970 to C.Y. Tung, a Hong Kong businessman, for conversion to a floating university in Hong Kong under the name of *Seawise University*.

After a much-delayed fit-out programme, in which boiler malfunctions had plagued the new liner, *Queen Elizabeth 2* finally departed on her maiden voyage on 30 May 1969. The new ship had a very different exterior profile, with a single, stylised mast and a thin white-and-black funnel, without the traditional Cunard red. Internally she was modern, with interior spaces that made use of chrome, aluminium, fibreglass and leather. A two-class ship during her transatlantic crossings, she operated as a single-class ship for cruises.

QE2, as the new ship became affectionately known, proved very popular, and became the longest lasting of the dual-purpose liners that were introduced at the time. In fact, she was so popular that Cunard were able to start repaying the government loan they had acquired for her construction in her first year of service.

The Columbia Restaurant aboard *QE2* was for first-class passengers. (Cunard/ Michael Gallagher)

Above and below: The Lookout Bar aboard *QE2* was the only forward facing bar aboard the ship, and sported a very 'swinging '60s' decor. (Cunard/Michael Gallagher)

QE2's Lookout Bar was removed during her first refit to make room for a galley. (Cunard/Michael Gallagher)

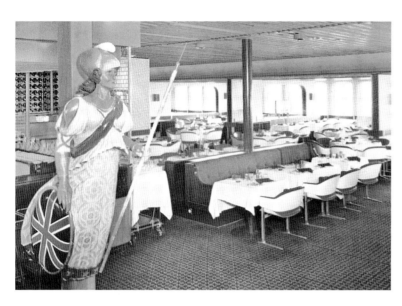

The Britannia restaurant was *QE2*'s tourist-class dining room. (Cunard/Michael Gallagher)

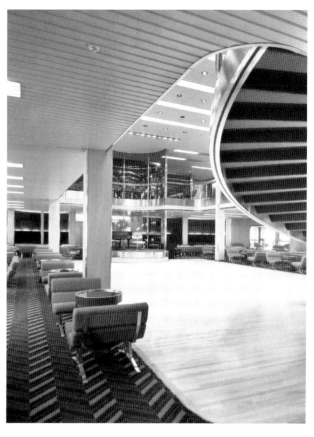

QE2's Double Down Room sported a spiral staircase, double-height ceilings and a large dance floor. (Cunard/Michael Gallagher)

With black walls, chrome balustrades and green leather chairs, *QE2*'s Midships Lobby was futuristic and modern. (Cunard/Michael Gallagher)

The Queens Room was *QE2*'s first-class lounge. (Cunard/Michael Gallagher)

The *QE2* was both a liner and a cruise ship, and is seen here berthed during a cruise. (Cunard/Michael Gallagher)

Below: *QE2* at rest during an early cruise. In 1972 the first change to her profile was made, with the addition of balcony accomodation to her top decks and the removal of the Lookout Bar. (Cunard/Michael Gallagher)

▶ DID YOU KNOW?

In 1974, *Caribia*, the former *Caronia*, was sold for scrap, having been mostly laid up since her withdrawal from Cunard. During the voyage under tow to Taiwan, *Caribia* was wrecked off the coast of Guam.

10

TRAFALGAR HOUSE OWNERSHIP

Cunard's cruising activity is complementary to [our] Caribbean hotel developments.

Trafalgar House statement on the purchase of Cunard Line

With the *QE2* settled into regular service, Cunard set about streamlining the business further in order to allow them to repay the government loan. *QE2* proved to be a very popular ship. The new *Queen* was a vast departure from traditional Cunard liners; and was very popular with younger ocean travellers.

Seven years prior to *QE2*'s entry into service, the Trafalgar House Co., a fledgling property development firm, was establishing itself in London. Under the leadership of a young Sir Nigel Broakes, the organisation grew quickly and by the early 1970s the London Stock Exchange-listed company was acquiring a variety of assets. As part of its seemingly unstoppable expansion, Trafalgar House acquired Cunard Line in 1971. With the acquisition came the Cunard fleet, which included *QE2*, *Franconia* and *Carmania*, as well as a cargo fleet of over forty vessels.

At the time of the acquisition, Cunard also had two cruise ships with a gross tonnage (gt) of 14,194 on order. Originally designed as the first two of eight vessels for Overseas National Airways, the *Cunard Adventurer* and *Cunard Ambassador* entered service in 1971 and 1972 respectively. With the anticipated arrival of the new tonnage, *Franconia* and *Carmania* were withdrawn from service. This saw a brief end to Cunard's dedicated presence in the Caribbean.

Since 1967 Cunard had contributed to the joint-venture container line, ACL. As part of their commitment to this collaboration, the line operated two of ACL's roll-on roll-off container ships. These vessels, *Atlantic Conveyor* and *Atlantic Causeway*, each carried wheeled vehicles as well as containers and were built by Swan Hunter in Newcastle upon Tyne.

With the exception of the ACL venture, Trafalgar House moved to divest the Cunard freight business, leaving Cunard to concentrate on passenger operations. *QE2* was given a £1 million refurbishment in 1972, which included the addition of balcony suites to her Signal and Sports decks. This made *QE2* one of the first passenger ships to offer balcony cabins.

QE2 was the subject of a bomb scare in 1972 while on an eastbound transatlantic crossing. Following a telephoned threat, the ship's security team, under the command of Captain Law, swept the vessel and found nothing. Nevertheless, the threat was taken seriously, and a team of highly trained members of the British SAS were parachuted Into the sea near QE2. Once aboard the ship, they performed their own search but no bomb was found. The event turned out to be a hoax and the culprit was later arrested for making similar threats to American Airlines.

In 1975, QE2 undertook her maiden world cruise. Her dual-purpose design made her the perfect vessel for long-distance cruising, while the 963ft length of the ship meant that, unlike the previous Queens, QE2 could transit the Panama Canal. The ninety-two-day voyage saw QE2 visit twenty-three ports and complete her first full circumnavigation of the globe.

Cunard's Trafalgar years were characterised by expansion of services across a diverse range of markets. The first major step in this programme was the acquisition of further tonnage. Two new cruise ships of around 17,000-gt, each with the capacity to carry over 940 passengers, were added to the fleet in the mid-1970s. Named Cunard Countess and Cunard Princess, the vessels were originally designed with input from Playboy founder Hugh Heffner. Intended to be floating playgrounds, the ships were to sail for the MGM brand.

With Cunard's acquisition of the ships during the building process, their design was tweaked to become two of the most successful early 4-star cruise ships. From 1976, Cunard positioned the Cunard Countess in the Caribbean, while Cunard Princess entered service in 1977 and concentrated mainly on the Mediterranean market, as well as occasional voyages to Bermuda and Alaska.

In 1982, four ships in Cunard's fleet were requisitioned for use during the Falklands War. This included QE2, which was called up on 3 May. The QE2 was at sea when the announcement was made and the ship's captain and officers actually heard about the ship's requisition via BBC Radio 2 before they were officially advised by Cunard.

QE2's transformation for wartime use was dramatic, with the ship's aft decks being cut away to add a heli-deck; while her decks were strengthened with the addition of steel plating. At the end of the eight-day refurbishment, QE2 set sail for the South Atlantic. Aboard the ship were 3,000 troops from the 5th Infantry Brigade, comprising the Scots Guards, the Welsh Guards and Gurkhas.

During the campaign, QE2 was purposely kept out of the warzone, staying in the relative safety of Cumberland Bay. There, she transferred her troops to other ships, including the P&O liner Canberra. QE2 then took on survivors from the HMS Ardent, HMS Coventry and HMS Antelope

before sailing back to Southampton. The ship arrived at Southampton on 11 June 1982 and was met by the Royal Yacht Britannia with HM the Queen Mother aboard who sent QE2 a special message of congratulations.

The Cunard-operated ACL vessels Atlantic Conveyor and Atlantic Causeway were also requisitioned for use during the Falklands War. They were particularly useful for the war effort due to their unique design as both container ship and roll-on roll-off carrier. Both ships were used to carry RAF helicopters and Sea Harriers as well as vehicles and cargo supplies for the war effort. While Atlantic Causeway successfully returned home at the end of the campaign, Atlantic Conveyor was not so lucky. She was attacked on 25 May by an Argentine Dassault-Breguet Super Étendard jet, which fired two Exocet missiles into the ship. She burnt out with the loss of twelve crewmembers, including her captain. She was later taken under tow but sunk shortly afterwards.

At the end of the conflict in October 1982, the Cunard Countess was requisitioned for use by the government. She was used for troop movements between Ascension Island and Port Stanley while the airfield was repaired from damage sustained during the conflict. Cunard Countess also undertook a special voyage carrying families of those lost during the war to the South Atlantic for a commemorative ceremony.

At the end of their service, each of the surviving Cunard ships was given an extensive refit; QE2's was undertaken in Southampton and included the addition of the first Golden Door Spa at Sea. Cunard Countess' refit contract was awarded to a shipyard in Malta, which caused an outcry among nationalists in Great Britain.

In 1983, Cunard's fleet was again expanded when Trafalgar House purchased Norwegian America Line. The purchase included two of the highest-rated ships afloat: Sagafjord and Vistafjord. Both were renowned among 5-star travellers, and boasted a fiercely loyal clientele. After considering renaming the ships to re-establish the traditional 'ia' naming convention, it was decided to retain their Norwegian names, as well as their Norwegian crew.

With their funnels repainted in the Cunard colours and initially operating under the Cunard-NAL sub-brand, Sagafjord and Vistafjord retained their popularity. Sagafjord undertook annual world cruises while Vistafjord's itineraries concentrated mainly on the European luxury cruise market.

Trafalgar House further grew Cunard's fleet in 1986, when the company purchased the ailing Sea Goddess Line. Sea Goddess had run into financial hardship after completing the first two luxury yachts in what was to be a series of eight ships. With this acquisition, Cunard formed the Cunard-Sea Goddess sub-brand and placed these two highly rated ships into operation.

That same year, QE2's service-life expectancy was extended with a mammoth reengineering project. The ship's steam turbines had been troublesome since she entered service and by the mid-1980s were creating significant issues for the ship. Thus, US$100 million was spent on what was the largest and most complex marine propulsion transformation programme in history.

The works, which were completed at the Lloyd Werft shipyard in Bremerhaven, Germany, included the removal of QE2's entire steam propulsion system, which amounted to 4,700 tons of material. This was replaced with an entirely new diesel electric system comprising nine medium-speed MAN-B&W engines, each weighing 220 tons.

The ship's funnel was removed to facilitate the extraction of her old power plant as well as the installation of the new engines. These diesels created power, which fed two gigantic British-built propulsion motors – the largest ever constructed for a merchant vessel.

During QE2's refurbishment programme, Sagafjord replaced her on the transatlantic crossings, maintaining Cunard's regular presence on this route. Sagafjord proved very popular on this route, and her voyages enjoyed strong bookings.

QE2 returned to commercial service in April 1987, with her first voyage being a short trip along the Solent. Aboard was HRH Princess Diana along with a group of local underprivileged children.

In 1989 the Cunard flagship was chartered twice for use in Japan. The first charter was for seventy-five days, in honour of the 130th anniversary of the city of Yokohama. The second lasted six months, with QE2 docked in Osaka for the World Exposition. During QE2's charters, Vistafjord was used as Cunard's transatlantic liner. Vistafjord had originally been built with transatlantic crossings in mind, and her use in this role proved popular both with passengers and her crew. Vistafjord also offered unique

CAPTAIN LAW'S ADDRESS TO QE2 PASSENGERS DURING THE 1972 BOMB SCARE

Ladies and Gentlemen, we have received information concerning a threat of a bomb-explosion on board this ship some time during this voyage.

We have received such threats in the past, which have so far turned out to be hoaxes. However, we always take them seriously and take every possible precaution.

On this occasion we are being assisted by the British Government who are sending out bomb disposal experts who will be parachuted into the sea and picked up by boat and brought aboard.

I will of course keep you fully informed about the situation. Cunard are taking every precaution ashore and on board and will take any necessary action to minimise risk. If there is any question of it being necessary to pay over money, this will be done ashore in New York.

I can only ask you to remain calm. On these occasions lots of rumours tend to circulate.

Please only take notice of any information that comes from me directly or from one of my officers. That is all for the moment.

QE2 departing New York in her original colour scheme. (Cunard/Michael Gallagher)

itineraries, including a voyage to the Amazon, and a forty-day cruise to the Mediterranean, which departed from the American cruising hub of Fort Lauderdale.

The beginning of the 1990s was characterised by further expansion. Trafalgar House added European river vessels, including the renowned *Mozart* and *Dresden*, to the Cunard stable, as well as hotel management. In fact, Cunard were operating the Ritz Hotel in London for Trafalgar House.

In 1993, Cunard's fleet expanded again with a joint venture with the Crown Cruise Line. Crown had been operating three new ships, which now sailed as *Cunard Crown Monarch*, *Cunard Crown Jewel* and *Cunard Crown Dynasty* under the Cunard-Crown sub-brand. *Cunard Countess* and *Cunard Princess* were moved under the Cunard-Crown banner, although their original names were retained.

While *Cunard Crown Jewel* and *Cunard Crown Dynasty* were popular ships, the line made an error in sending *Cunard Crown Monarch* to Australia. Australian cruising had been dominated by Sitmar's (later P&O Holidays') *Fairstar* for many years. *Fairstar* offered cheap, informal cruises from Sydney to the South Pacific, which was perfect for the fledgling Australian cruise market. *Cunard Crown Monarch*'s more sophisticated and expensive voyages were unappealing to the local market at the time and the ship was withdrawn and sold in 1994.

That year saw the final Trafalgar House-controlled addition to the Cunard fleet. *Royal Viking Sun* was the flagship of the Royal Viking Line, which Trafalgar acquired and merged with Cunard. The line created yet another sub-brand, Cunard Royal Viking, which operated *Royal Viking Sun* along with *Sagafjord* and *Vistafjord*. The addition of *Royal Viking* meant Cunard's passenger fleet reached its largest size since the introduction of the jet. However, the mismatched fleet, sprawling hotel and river-cruise operation was difficult to control, expensive to market and ultimately unprofitable.

Trafalgar House took a number of steps to try and stem the losses at Cunard. These included a restructure of the line, as well as a multi-million-pound refurbishment of *QE2* in order to revitalise her public areas. While *QE2*'s refit resulted in a dramatic and ultimately very popular transformation of the liner, the work aboard the ship overran the schedule with construction still underway when *QE2* sailed on her December 1994 voyage. This was a public relations disaster for the line as the negative press associated with the voyage lasted well into the new year.

By the end of *QE2*'s 1995 world cruise her reputation had been restored; however, Cunard's finances kept deteriorating. During that year the line posted a £16 million loss. This resulted in a further restructure of the line, which included the ageing *Sagafjord* being flagged for retirement from Cunard service in 1996. *Sagafjord* had not enjoyed the same care as *Vistafjord* and had missed several scheduled refurbishments, which had impacted on her 5-star plus rating. Her removal from the fleet had been expected for several months before the official announcement was made. Other tonnage departed during 1995, including *Cunard Princess* and *Cunard Crown Jewel*, which were both sold, leaving the Cunard Crown fleet diminished to just two ships.

The cost of maintaining sub-brands took a further toll on Cunard's finances and by 1997 *Cunard Countess* and *Cunard Crown Dynasty* had also left the fleet.

By 1998, Cunard's fleet had been reduced to five ships. The mismatched fleet was plagued by the company's lack of funds. Trafalgar House had by this time been acquired by Kværner, which sought a buyer for the ailing Cunard Line.

Cunard Adventurer and *Cunard Ambassador* were used for cruising. (Bill Miller)

Cunard Adventurer (pictured) and *Cunard Ambassador* were given the same black and white funnel colours as *QE2*. (Tee Adams)

Looking up at *QE2*'s original funnel. (Tee Adams)

An aerial shot of the world's most iconic floating resort, *QE2*. (Cunard/Michael Gallagher)

Cunard Princess was originally to be named 'Cunard Conquest'. (Tee Adams)

Rob Lightbody runs the well-known *QE2* Story website and has had a long connection with Cunard's longest serving flagship:

For years, in the 1970s and '80s, my dad would disappear off to faraway lands 'to fix the *QE2*'. We knew what she was – she was famous and on TV often – but I didn't truly understand what she was until I went aboard, first as a child, then as an adult. She was the most special, amazing, beautiful ship in the world. The seven seas are a bit less interesting without *QE2* sailing upon them.

▶ DID YOU KNOW?

Royal Viking Sun did not stay with Seabourn for long. In 2002, she was moved to Holland America and was renamed *Prinsendam*.

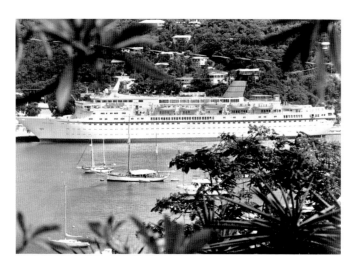

Left: *Cunard Countess* was Cunard's Caribbean cruise ship. (Ronald W. Warwick; *QE2*: The Cunard Flagship Queen Elizabeth 2)

QE2 refuels at sea during her service in the Falklands War. (Ronald W. Warwick; *QE2*: The Cunard Flagship Queen Elizabeth 2)

Above: A sea king helicopter departs from *QE2*'s aft decks during the Falklands War. (Ronald W. Warwick; *QE2*: The Cunard Flagship Queen Elizabeth 2)

Left: *QE2* in Philadelphia in April 1982, shortly before her Falklands service. The Walt Whitman bridge, between Pennsylvania and New Jersey, can be seen behind, as well as a Curtis Bay tug. (Tee Adams)

QE2's bow was converted into a helipad for her service in the Falklands War. (Ronald W. Warwick; *QE2*: The Cunard Flagship Queen Elizabeth 2)

Below: *QE2* undergoes her post-war refurbishment. (Ronald W. Warwick; *QE2*: The Cunard Flagship Queen Elizabeth 2)

Upon returning to Southampton, *QE2* was greeted by Queen Elizabeth, The Queen Mother aboard the Royal Yacht *Britannia*. (Cunard/Michael Gallagher)

QE2 in her grey hull, her post-war colour scheme. (Tee Adams)

The pebble grey hull was difficult to maintain. (Ronald W. Warwick; QE2: The Cunard Flagship Queen Elizabeth 2)

By 1984 QE2's hull had once more been painted in the darker federal grey. (Tee Adams)

Vistafjord commanded a loyal following. (Bill Miller)

QE2's profile just prior to her 1986/87 refurbishment. This image shows the original funnel and Magrodome open over the Quarter Deck pool. (Cunard/ Michael Gallagher)

 DID YOU KNOW?

In 1971, QE2 came to the aid of the French ship Antilles, which had run aground off the coast of Mustique.

QE2's steam turbine engines were replaced with diesels, pictured here. (Frame/Cross)

Cunard's *Sea Goddess I* and *II* together. (Bill Miller)

Princess Diana aboard QE2 in 1987 for a charity cruise. (Cunard/Michael Gallagher)

Margaret Thatcher aboard QE2 to honour the ship's service during the Falklands. (Cunard/ Michael Gallagher)

Queen Elizabeth The Queen Mother speaks aboard QE2. (Cunard/Michael Gallagher)

QE2's rendezvous with the Royal Yacht *Britannia*. (Cunard/Michael Gallagher)

HM the Queen aboard QE2 in 1990. (Cunard/Michael Gallagher)

Cunard Crown Monarch failed to capture the Australian market. (Bill Miller)

Sagafjord was built for Norwegian America Line. She was a dual purpose liner, but from early in her career concentrated on cruising. (Bill Miller)

Sagafjord off Cayman in 1995. *Sagafjord* was a classic liner with a 5-star rating. (Tee Adams)

In 1994 Cunard acquired the 5-star *Royal Viking Sun*. (Bill Miller)

QE2 passes the World Trade Centre following her 1994 refurbishment. (Cunard/Michael Gallagher)

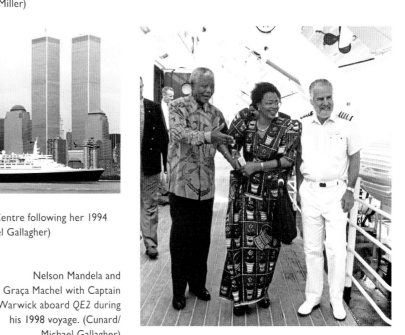

Nelson Mandela and Graça Machel with Captain Warwick aboard *QE2* during his 1998 voyage. (Cunard/ Michael Gallagher)

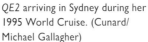

QE2 arriving in Sydney during her 1995 World Cruise. (Cunard/ Michael Gallagher)

QE2 wore the golden lion and speed stripe on her superstructure after her 1994 refit. (Frame/Cross)

11

CARNIVAL OWNERSHIP

Our goal is nothing less than to create a new Golden Age of sea travel for those who missed the first.

Cunard President and COO Larry Pimintel on Project Queen Mary

Cunard's fortunes changed dramatically in April 1998. After months of turmoil, the 158-year-old company finally had a buyer in the giant Carnival Corporation. Carnival Corporation had commenced operations as a small cruise line in 1972. The brainchild of American immigrant Ted Arison, the line's approach was to offer fun, cheap cruises departing from US ports such as Miami and Fort Lauderdale.

With a fleet of converted former ocean liners, the early days were turbulent; with the first ship, *Mardi Gras*, running aground during her maiden voyage. However, their business model and marketing position was strong, and Carnival grew to become the dominant player in the youth cruise market. The success of the line allowed it to acquire existing brands. Today the company owns a vast number of cruise ship operators, including P&O Cruises, Costa, Holland America, Seabourn, Princess, AIDA and Cunard.

Despite the size and scale of Carnival, the merchant shipping industry, by and large, were genuinely surprised at the Cunard acquisition. Other lines, such as P&O and Princess (which at the time were not part of Carnival), had looked at Cunard and deemed the company as something of a lost cause. However, Carnival's head, Micky Arison (son of Ted), could see the value in Cunard that no other shipping operator could – the value of its brand.

By late 1998 plans were well underway for the company's transformation, which was enacted the following year. Under the leadership of new president and COO Larry Pimintel, the now Miami-based Cunard set about reinventing itself.

QE2 and *Vistafjord* were both given extensive refurbishments. *QE2*'s refit cost over US$30 million, and included the completion of outstanding interior design work from the 1994 refit, as well as a complete hull strip and repaint back into traditional Cunard colours.

Vistafjord was also treated to an extensive refit, and emerged with a new name – *Caronia*. The name change came with a new feel for the ship, and although *Caronia* retained many of the features that her repeat guests

Far left: Repainted in traditional Cunard livery, QE2 and Caronia shared millennium eve together. (Cunard/Michael Gallagher)

Left: QM2 was built using prefabricated blocks. Here you can see them being prepared at the shipyard. (Pam Massey)

Far left: The yet-to-be-painted QM2 is taking shape. You can see the mast on the dockside, awaiting installation. (Pam Massey)

Left: The name Queen Mary 2 has been attached and is prepared for painting. (Pam Massey)

loved, she was given a very British treatment during the refit. This was a deliberate move, aimed at standardising the Cunard fleet to allow the line to re-establish itself in a niche market.

The remaining vessels in the Cunard fleet – Royal Viking Sun, Sea Goddess I and Sea Goddess II – were transferred into the Carnival-owned Seabourn fleet and renamed Seabourn Sun, Seabourn Goddess I and Seabourn Goddess II. Seabourn had been merged with Cunard in 1998 to form Cunard Line Ltd, a holding company that operated both the Cunard and Seabourn brands. A variety of functions were shared, including websites built off the same design and commonality across brochures and branding.

On 8 June 1999, Larry Pimentel announced the company's intention to build the first transatlantic liner since QE2 was launched in 1967. The news was met with great surprise from those in the industry. Of the plans, Pimentel told excited reporters that:

The project will lead to development of the heaviest liner ever built; the epitome of elegance, style and grace … It is our objective to build a new generation of ocean liner that will be the very pinnacle of the shipbuilder's art; the realization of a dream of another time … Our goal is nothing less than to create a new Golden Age of sea travel for those who missed the first.

QM2 in Southampton for the first time, in December 2003. (Andy Fitzsimmons)

HM the Queen and Commodore R.W. Warwick aboard QM2. (Commodore R.W. Warwick)

QE2 and QM2 met in New York for the first time in April 2004. (Thad Constantine)

The first official meeting of the planning and design team followed the official announcement. Under the direction of chief naval architect Stephen Payne, the design evolved from a ship of similar dimensions to QE2, to become the longest, largest, tallest, widest and most expensive passenger ship ever built at the time.

There were a variety of reasons why the new liner, codenamed 'Project Queen Mary', was so large. The driving factor for the size was the requirement for a high percentage of balcony accommodation aboard the ship. This was the first ocean liner ever designed with such a requirement and the design team had to think laterally about how this would be achieved, resulting in the creation of sheltered veranda cabins, or 'hull holes', that sat beneath the boat deck.

Other considerations were taken into the design, which added to the ship's bulk. A long streamlined bow, hydrodynamic hull and terraced aft decks became the signatures of the ship's external appearace, while internally the ship was given the largest ballroom at sea, a full-size planetarium and the magnificent multi-storey Britannia Restaurant.

While much of Cunard's attention was devoted to building their new ship, QE2 and Caronia were enjoying ever-increasing popularity. With the refurbishment work complete, the two ships offered a series of voyages from Southampton, while QE2 maintained her transatlantic schedule. Both vessels celebrated New Year's Eve 1999 off Barbados. Aboard both

Cunarders there was much talk of Project Queen Mary, with particular discussion among passengers and crew over which shipyard would build the new liner, with many traditionalists hoping the work would go to a British yard.

Following a tender process, the French shipyard Chantiers de l'Atlantique was selected to build the new Cunard liner. John Brown, the Scottish yard responsible for the original Queens, had long since shut down, while Harland & Wolff were unsuccessful in their bid for the work. The French shipyard had a pedigree of building ocean liners, having constructed the Normandie and France, as well as owning a fitting-out basin and gantry large enough to accommodate the massive new liner. The letter of intent was signed on 10 March 2000, while the formal contracts were signed in November that same year.

The devastating terrorist attacks of 11 September 2001 impacted Cunard; with the QE2 en route to New York at the time of the attacks, the Cunard flagship was diverted to Boston due to the closure of New York to shipping. Boston became the American home for QE2 until she returned to New York in January 2002, making her the first cruise ship to return to the port.

The keel-laying ceremony for Project Queen Mary took place on 4 July 2002. The construction of the new Cunard liner was extremely fast, and only a fraction of the time taken to build the previous Cunard Queens.

This was largely thanks to the adoption of prefabrication in the building process, where large pre-made blocks were assembled to create the finished ship.

On 30 May 2003, Cunard and Saga Holidays announced that Saga had bought *Caronia* with the intention of operating the ship in conjunction with her former fleet mate *Sagafjord*, now *Saga Rose*. Despite the purchase occurring in 2003, *Caronia* remained in the Cunard fleet until late 2004, allowing for a well-patronised farewell season.

Also in 2003, Cunard announced their intention to build an 80,000-gt cruise ship. To be named *Queen Victoria*, the new vessel's hull was laid down on 12 July 2003 at the Fincanteri yards in Italy. The new vessel was of the 'Vista' class, having originally been allocated to Holland America line. On 22 December 2003 Chantiers de l'Atlantique completed Project Queen Mary and the ship was handed over to Cunard Line. After a shakedown cruise under the command of Commodore Ronald W. Warwick, the ship arrived in Southampton where HM Queen Elizabeth II officially named her *Queen Mary 2* (*QM2*) on 8 January 2004.

That same month, *QE2* departed on her final world cruise as Cunard's flagship. After a three-month circumnavigation of the globe, the venerable Cunarder rendezvoused with the newer, larger *QM2* in New York, creating much attention. Following a full day side by side, the two Queens departed New York for a tandem transatlantic crossing to Southampton. Upon their arrival, *QM2* officially became flagship of the Cunard fleet.

In mid-2004, Cunard announced that they had transferred ownership of the incomplete *Queen Victoria* to sister-brand P&O Cruises. Renamed *Arcadia*, the vessel was floated out on 26 June 2004 and entered service in March the following year.

The reason for the change was linked to the success of *QM2*. Cunard had identified a niche luxury market for passengers wishing to sail aboard ocean liners, as evidenced by *QM2*'s popularity since her introduction into service as well as the ongoing loyalty of passengers to *QE2* and *Caronia*. To that end, a new *Queen Victoria* was ordered in December 2004 from Fincanteri. Although based on the 'Vista'-class design, the new liner was altered to include some ocean-liner traits. Her bow and forward superstructure were strengthened, allowing her to undertake occasional transatlantic crossings; while the hull was lengthened to create space for a ballroom – a hallmark of previous Cunard Queens. In the words of Cunard Line at the time, the new vessel would 'adhere to the grand ocean liner design inspired by current vessels *QE2* and *QM2*'.

QM2's funnel, based on that aboard *QE2*, includes a wind scoop at the base to direct smoke away from the aft decks. (Frame/Cross)

QM2 was the first ship to have a planetarium. The large dome retracts into the ceiling above allowing the room to be used for a variety of purposes. (Frame/Cross)

QM2's Costanzi stern blends the elegance of a curved cruiser stern with the hydrodynamic efficiency of a transom stern. (Frame / Cross)

Left: The *QM2* arrives in Long Beach California. (Nick Souza)

Centre left: *QE2* follows the outbound *QM2* down Southampton Water. (Cunard/Michael Gallagher)

Bottom left: *QM2* meets *Queen Mary* in Long Beach. (Nick Souza)

Right: *QM2* manoeuvres in the harbour after her rendezvous with the original *Queen Mary* in Long Beach, California. (Nick Souza)

Below: *QE2* with the new *Queen Victoria* at Fort Lauderdale. (Cunard/Michael Gallagher)

Queen Victoria was floated out on 15 January 2007, and entered service with Cunard that December. The ship quickly filled the gap left by Caronia's departure, and introduced a new group of cruisers to Cunard's fleet.

That same year, the Cunard community was shocked at the announcement of QE2's retirement. The 38-year-old liner was enjoying ongoing popularity and it had been widely expected that a proposed refurbishment would keep the liner in service for several years to come. However, this was not to be. Instead, QE2 was sold to Dubai World for a sum of US$100 million. Fortunately for QE2's loyal following there was time to say goodbye, with the official retirement date not until November 2008.

On 13 January 2008, the three Queens met in New York harbour in the first of many celebratory events designed to bid QE2 a farewell, and establish Queen Victoria and QM2 as her successors. This event was followed by a further rendezvous of QE2 and Queen Victoria in Sydney harbour, which mirrored a similar event the previous year when QE2 met QM2 in the Australian city.

In October 2008, QE2 and QM2 undertook a special farewell tandem transatlantic crossing. Travelling both westbound and then eastbound, the event allowed America to say farewell to QE2 for the final time before the ship was retired in November.

With QE2 gone, Cunard continued with plans to create a new Queen Elizabeth. Originally announced in 2007, the new liner was of similar design to Queen Victoria, albeit slightly larger at just over 90,900 gt.

In 2009, Carnival UK opened a new custom-built headquarters in Southampton called Carnival House. With the opening of this building, Cunard's management was relocated into the premises, which also houses a number of other Carnival Corporation brands. In this new working environment, resources between the various brands are shared, with Cunard Line operating in increasingly close ties with P&O Cruises.

In late 2010, the new Queen Elizabeth was handed over to Cunard at a ceremony held by the Fincanteri shipyard. Named on 11 October 2010, by HM Queen Elizabeth II, the ship entered service the following day and went on to establish herself in the Mediterranean cruise market.

Queen Victoria's funnel was inspired by QE2. (Frame/Cross)

ROYAL RENDEZVOUS: QM2 AND QE2 IN SYDNEY

The date 20 February 2007 is one the people of Sydney won't soon forget. On this day the city was brought to a standstill by the meeting of two great ocean liners.

QM2 arrived in Sydney early that morning, making her maiden visit during her inaugural world cruise. The ship, under the command of Captain (later Commodore) Christopher Rynd, performed a 180° manoeuvre near the Sydney Harbour Bridge before docking at the nearby naval base.

During the day, the harbour and surrounding areas became increasingly crowded as people awaited the arrival of QE2. The event had been well marketed, as it was the first time that two Cunard Queens had been together in Sydney since the Second World War.

By the time QE2 arrived in the harbour late that afternoon, a crowd estimated at well over a million people had descended on Sydney. The city was in complete gridlock, with traffic jams lasting well into the night.

QE2 and *Queen Victoria* make for an impressive sight alongside the Sydney Opera House. (Cunard/Michael Gallagher)

QE2 and *Queen Victoria* met in Sydney harbour in 2008. *QE2* was on her final world cruise, while *Queen Victoria* was making her maiden. (Cunard/Michael Gallagher)

Bill Miller is a well-known maritime author and lecturer and has had a long affection for the Cunard Line:

As a youngster, watching ships and especially the great liners, in New York harbour, I think the Cunard liners were my favourites. They were the epitome of what great ocean liners were and should be. They were big, immaculate, regal, and capped by those wonderful orange-red and black funnels.

In the 1950s, there might be as many as four Cunard liners in port, at Piers 90 & 92, within a week. Tuesday and Wednesday were, of course, the traditional days for the Queens – one of them was over-nighting in port. And, of course, the Cunard offices in Lower Manhattan, at the bottom end of Broadway in the shipping district, were the grandest. It was, in ways, like visiting a great English country house – there was this extraordinary grandeur.

The Cunard Line was prestige, history, absolute magic in those days – and remain so to this day.

▶ DID YOU KNOW?

QE2 remains the longest-serving express liner in history, travelling more than 5.6 million miles over 39½ years.

Far left: *QE2* and *Queen Victoria* rendezvous in Sydney. (Cunard/ Michael Gallagher)

Left: *QE2*'s penultimate departure from New York, 2008. (Tee Adams)

The end of an era. The world's most beloved liner docked at Southampton for the last time. (Andy Fitzsimmons)

The legendary *QE2* departs Southampton for the last time. She was given a brilliant send off which culminated in a stunning fireworks display. (Andy Fitzsimmons)

QE2 arrived in Dubai on 26 November 2008. The following day, the Red Ensign was lowered for the last time when she was transferred to her new owners. (Gavin Harper)

Far left: Baggage lined up in Dubai at the end of *QE2*'s final voyage. (Gavin Harper)

Left: Vista Queens: *Queen Victoria* (right) meets *Queen Elizabeth* (left). (Andrew Sassoli-Walker)

12

THE THREE QUEENS

Our flagship *Queen Mary 2* will recreate history when she sails from Liverpool on 4 July 2015, following in the wake of *Britannia* which left the city 175 years earlier to the day.

Cunard Line on the 175th anniversary celebrations

With the 2010 introduction of the third Cunarder to hold the name *Queen Elizabeth*, the line entered into a new, modern era. The years since Carnival purchased the line had seen Cunard reinvent itself, having replaced all of their tonnage with three new, large ships.

2010 was also a milestone year for Cunard with the appointment of the line's first female captain. Inger Klein Olsen (now Thorhauge) joined Cunard in 1997 as First Officer aboard *Vistafjord*. She later spent time working with Seabourn, rising in the ranks before returning to Cunard as Deputy Captain aboard *Queen Victoria* in August 2010. She was appointed Master in December 2010.

In 2011 *QM2*'s popularity soared following the eruption of Iceland's Eyjafjallajökull volcano. With transatlantic and European aircraft grounded, Cunard's flagship was the only way to travel between Britain and America. A waiting list of over 1,000 people developed for crossings aboard the Cunarder in the weeks following the eruption.

Cunard had been investigating the concept of weddings at sea for some time, however, legislation relating to the vessels' British registration prohibited this. Cunard's 2011 decision to re-register their fleet in Hamilton, Bermuda, opened the door for weddings to be held aboard their ships, although it did end a 171-year tradition of registering their ships in Great Britain.

Cunard made the switch commencing with *Queen Elizabeth* on 24 October 2011. *Queen Victoria* followed on 27 October while *QM2*'s registration was switched on 1 December 2011. As a result of the move, the vessels' registration letters changed, ending the use of Cunard's traditional registration letters of GBTT, which had been used for the original *Queen Mary*, *QE2* and the new *Queen Elizabeth*.

On 27 April 2012, *QM2* welcomed aboard former President George H. Bush and his wife. The couple were taking a transatlantic voyage back to the United States aboard the Cunard flagship. Cunard's President and

Managing Director Peter Shanks used the occasion to pay tribute to the line's longest serving senior officer, John Duffy, who served with Cunard for almost forty-seven years.

With 2012 marking the sixtieth anniversary of HM Queen Elizabeth II's coronation, the Cunard fleet was back in the spotlight. The Queen has a unique relationship with Cunard, being the only person known to have been present at the launch of all three Cunard ships to carry the name *Queen Elizabeth*.

On 5 June, in a special tribute event, the three Cunarders met in Southampton. With *Queen Elizabeth* and *Queen Victoria* docked, the flagship *QM2* arrived, sailing past her fleet mates carrying a large banner, which read 'Congratulations Ma'am'. The event attracted large crowds and a flyover by the RAF's Red Arrows, the first such flyover display in Southampton.

That same year, Cunard celebrated the fifth anniversary of *Queen Victoria*'s entry into service. To mark the occasion, Camilla, Duchess of Cornwall, visited the ship she had christened in 2007. The Duchess unveiled a portrait of herself, which was hung in the ship's Grand Lobby. The occasion was also used to mark a milestone in Cunard's relationship with the Princes' Trust charity, with Cunard guests having raised over £800,000.

Cunard has had a long association with Australia and New Zealand, particularly during the World Cruise season. Throughout the 1980s and 1990s, both *QE2* and *Sagafjord* were regular visitors to ports such as Auckland, Sydney and Fremantle.

With three *Queens* in service, Cunard's presence in the Southern Hemisphere has strengthened, and by 2012 all three *Queens* had spent time in Australian and New Zealand waters, voyages that proved very popular in the local market. In response to this popularity, *QM2* offered an extended circumnavigation of Australia in 2012. The voyage sold out within hours prompting the line to repeat the schedule in 2014.

The 2012-year ended with Cunard in the media, though this time the news centred on a former Cunard ship. *QE2*, which retired to Dubai in 2008 and had been in layup since arriving in the UAE, hit the headlines when *The Daily Mail* reported that the ship was to be sold for scrap.

The news relating to *QE2* was met by concerned Cunard loyalists, with many taking to Cunard's Facebook page to complain. In early 2013 Cunard confirmed via their social media channel that the rumours were untrue, with the ship remaining in layup at the Dubai Dry Dock.

For the first three months of 2013, both *QM2* and *Queen Victoria* were deployed on the annual World Cruise. *Queen Victoria* undertook a westbound voyage, taking in ports along the west coast of the US before

Queen Victoria and *Queen Elizabeth* (foreground) together in Fort Lauderdale. (Cunard/ Michael Gallagher)

Queen Elizabeth departing Fort Lauderdale for the first time. (Cunard/Michael Gallagher)

heading across the Pacific, while *QM2* sailed eastbound via Suez and Asia to Australia. *QM2*'s voyage included an extended circumnavigation of New Zealand, during which the giant liner visited the Milford Sound for the first time.

In July, *QM2* completed her 200th transatlantic crossing. The eastbound voyage was well subscribed, having sold out months in advance and included an array of special guests.

The year ended on a happy note, with Cunard announcing details of the 175th anniversary celebrations being prepared for 2015.

Cunard celebrated the tenth anniversary of *QM2* in 2014 with a series of special events. During her annual World Cruise, the ship made a number of maiden calls to celebrate her decade in service, while the three Cunarders met in both Lisbon and Southampton to mark the anniversary, drawing large crowds and reinforcing the popularity of Cunard.

When *QM2* arrived in Southampton she played host to the Duke of Edinburgh. Prince Philip was present at the naming of *QM2* and during his visit a decade later he was given a behind-the-scenes tour of the ship and met a number of her crew.

That October, *QM2* undertook a special voyage from Belgium to the United Kingdom during which she carried soil from a First World War battlefield in Flanders. It was the last of seventy bags containing soil from each of the Flanders battlefields and was later taken to the Flanders Field Memorial Garden in London.

As 2014 drew to a close, Cunard's attention became focused on its 175th anniversary, which promised to offer a series of memorable historic events, including a recreation of *Britannia*'s first voyage.

Vistas at sea: Queens *Elizabeth* and *Victoria*. (Cunard/Michael Gallagher)

Above and Right: *QM2*'s bow was inspired by earlier ocean liners. (Frame/Cross)

> **Christel Hansen is well known as the captain's secretary aboard *Queen Victoria*; however, she started her career aboard *Vistafjord*:**
>
> *Vistafjord* was a very homely and friendly ship, a really nice atmosphere. It was the perfect size – 700 passengers and 350 crew – and had very good itineraries (including three days in Sydney on one occasion).
>
> Most passengers came back again and again. We all were one big family. Those that know each other from back then (both passengers and crew) still have a special connection and so many good memories to share.
>
> I don't think I would have stayed at sea to begin with if it wasn't because I was on *Vistafjord*. It was silver service, true 5-star. It was a home away from home.

Left: QM2 seen in Gibraltar at close quarters with *Independence of the Seas*. (Frame/Cross)

Below: A standard oceanview cabin aboard *Queen Victoria* as seen in its original decor. (Frame/Cross)

Far Left: *Queen Elizabeth* all lit up at night during a 'meeting of the Queens' event in New York. (Cunard/Michael Gallagher)

Left: *Queen Victoria* near the New York skyscrapers. (Cunard/Michael Gallagher)

Below left: QM2 near the Statue of Liberty. (Cunard/Michael Gallagher)

Below right: *Queen Mary 2*, *Queen Victoria* and *Queen Elizabeth* pause in formation for a fireworks display. (Cunard/Michael Gallagher)

► **DID YOU KNOW?**

The iconic Cunard Building in Liverpool is now in use as office space and marketed The Cunard.

Above: *Queen Victoria* at anchor at the UNESCO-protected Geirangerfjord, Norway. (Frame/Cross)

Queen Elizabeth's bow and forward superstructure viewed from one of her tender boats while at anchor during a port day. (Frame/Cross)

Queen Mary 2 passes a pilot boat as she departs Southampton. This photo was taken from *Queen Victoria* during the 2015 Three Queens event. (Frame/Cross)

Author Sam Warwick reflects on his family's special connection with Cunard Line:

The Cunard Line has always been a big part of my life and features among some of my earliest childhood memories. Both my father Ron Warwick and grandfather William 'Bil' Warwick were Cunard Line commodores.

My grandfather, or 'Grandpa-Captain' as my sister and I used to fondly call him, commanded many famous Cunard liners including *Caronia*, *Queen Mary* and *Queen Elizabeth*. The pinnacle of his career was becoming the first master of the new *Queen Elizabeth 2* (*QE2*) and commanding the maiden voyage in 1969.

My father joined Cunard in 1970 and served on the *QE2* and many other Cunard vessels, ultimately also becoming captain of the *QE2* in 1990. History repeated itself when he was appointed Master Designate of the new *Queen Mary 2* (*QM2*) in 2002.

Numerous Warwick family members have served as officers and crew on Cunard ships in various capacities, including my grandmother Evelyn who was a hairdresser and my cousin Robert who was a navigator on *QE2*. Several significant family events have taken place on Cunard vessels such as my sister Rebecca's wedding on *QE2* and my daughter Elizabeth's christening on *QM2*.

A lifetime of personal Cunard adventures commenced with my first *QE2* Transatlantic crossing in 1975 at the age of 7. I have vivid memories of the voyage along with a certificate signed by Captain Jackson proclaiming me to be a 'sailor of first class quality'! As I grew up I was privileged to be able to have holidays aboard the *QE2*, *Cunard Princess* and *Cunard Countess*. As an adult, highlights have included the Millennium World Cruise on *QE2* and the inaugural voyages of *QM2*.

It was during a call to St Thomas on the *Cunard Countess* in 1992 that I first discovered scuba diving. A few years later I found myself diving on the wreck of the Cunard liner *Aurania* in the Sound of Mull off the west coast of Scotland. Learning more about the events surrounding the shipwreck proved the catalyst to research the final resting places of all Cunard vessels and to personally dive as many as possible. This included travelling to locations around the world including the British Isles, Newfoundland and Guam, culminating with the publication of *Shipwrecks of the Cunard Line* in 2012.

I am proud that I have been able to continue my own contribution to the Warwick family's long association with the Cunard Line by collaborating with my father on the fourth edition of his authoritative book *QE2: The Cunard Line Flagship Queen Elizabeth 2*.

▶ DID YOU KNOW?

In 2013, *QM2* came to the aid of rower Mylène Paquette, who was attempting to row solo across the Atlantic.

Queen Mary 2's Ocean Liner design is evident in this image taken in Southampton water. Note the Normandie style breakwater on her bow. (Frame/Cross)

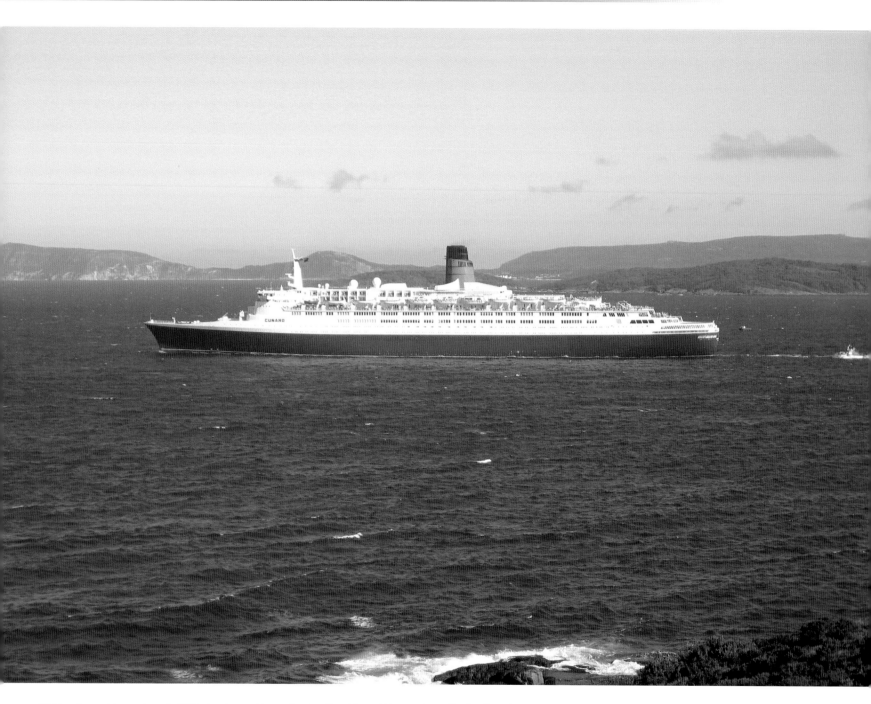

QE2 heading out to sea in early 2008 after her maiden and only call at Albany, Western Australia. (Jan Frame)

13

180 YEARS OF CUNARD

'Our new ship will be the first new Cunarder for 12 years.'

Cunard Line on the announcement of the new Pinnacle Class ship.

2015 marked Cunard's 175th anniversary year. A number of celebratory events, including various meetings of the Queens, were planned to celebrate this maritime milestone.

On 28 January 2015 *Queen Elizabeth* made her first call to Long Beach, California. Here she met the former Cunard Liner *Queen Mary*. The 90,400-gt *Queen Elizabeth* docked nearby, offering passengers the opportunity to visit the octogenarian ship.

Coinciding with this visit a Ship Model Gallery was opened aboard *Queen Mary*. Featuring large models of famous ocean liners, the gallery includes a builder's model of *Queen Mary*, as well as models of *QM2*, *QE2*, *Lusitania* and *Titanic*.

In addition to being Cunard's 175th anniversary year, 2015 was also the 100th anniversary of the tragic sinking of *Lusitania*. As such, in May a commemorative voyage departed Southampton bound for Ireland aboard *Queen Victoria*.

Dubbed '*Lusitania* Remembered', this cruise included a series of maritime history talks about *Lusitania* as well as a showcase of memorabilia and artefacts from the lost liner.

A key moment in the voyage took place in the early hours of 7 May as *Queen Victoria* passed over the site of *Lusitania*'s wreck. Passengers and crew braved the dark, and the cold May air to gather on deck and pay their respects. Wreaths were dropped into the water, while Commodore Rynd spoke solemn words of remembrance.

Later that morning, *Queen Victoria* came alongside in Cobh where a large service was held in the city. Speakers included Irish President Michael D. Higgins and Commodore Rynd, while prayers were led by the clergy.

Cunard's 175th anniversary celebrations attracted global media attention on 25 May 2015 when the Three Queens visited Liverpool for a historic rendezvous on the River Mersey.

Lusitania sunk off the coast of Cobh, Ireland in 1915. The city hosted a memorial service to mark the 100th anniversary on 7 May 2015. (Frame/Cross)

Queen Mary 2, which had been berthed at the Liverpool pier since the day before, sailed from her berth where she was joined by *Queen Elizabeth* and *Queen Victoria*. Together, the three ships approached the iconic Cunard Building, before performing a synchronised 360-degree turn.

Every vantage point was taken up by people eager to witness the spectacle, which also included the sounding of one, then seven, then five blasts on *QM2*'s whistle – in honour of the 175th anniversary.

For the event's finale the three ships lined up near the Cunard Building and remained in formation, just 420ft apart, as the Red Arrows performed an awe-inspiring low-level fly past, creating the perfect photo opportunity.

Queen Mary 2 took the celebrations to the USA and Canada when she sailed on a historic transatlantic crossing in July 2015. Departing Liverpool on 4 July, timed 175 years to the day of *Britannia*'s maiden departure, the Cunard flagship sailed to Halifax and Boston, recreating the original Cunard transatlantic service.

QM2's 10 July arrival in Halifax was met with an enthusiastic crowd. While the ship was alongside, Captain Kevin Oprey met with descendants of Sir Samuel Cunard.

Two days later the ship arrived in Boston. Here, senior members of *QM2*'s crew visited the former Boston Headquarters of Cunard, where a commemorative model of the *Servia* was gifted to the building.

Cunard's 175th anniversary ended with a royal visit while *QM2* was alongside in New York. Here, the ship hosted HRH The Princess Royal. This November 2015 luncheon aimed to raise money for HMS *Victory*, and was hosted by Cunard for the American Friends of the National Museum of the Royal Navy.

On a culinary note, in December Cunard replaced the Italian themed Todd English restaurants on *QM2* and *Queen Victoria* with the French inspired Verandah concept introduced on *Queen Elizabeth*. Verandah aimed to recreate the cuisine and ambiance of the Verandah Grill's found on the original *Queen Mary* and *Queen Elizabeth*, however, by 2019 the restaurants were offering a less Parisian menu, having morphed into steakhouse grills.

The major refurbishment of *QM2*, dubbed 'QM2 Remastered', dominated much of Cunard's attention in 2016. With the ship now 12 years old, the refit aimed to refresh and enhance the interior design, while also adding a number of new balcony cabins to the vessel.

Work was undertaken at the Blohm + Voss shipyard in Hamburg, with *QM2* arriving in the city on 27 May 2016. An estimated 10,000 people lined the banks of the River Elbe to watch as the ship was manoeuvred into the drydock.

Over US$130 million was spent on the refurbishment, which included the complete redesign of the Kings Court Restaurant, as well as the creation of Café Carinthia in the space previously used as the Winter Garden.

Further aesthetic updates included a new colour palette in both the Queens and Princess Grill restaurants; the re-carpeting of every cabin and the reupholstering of furniture throughout the ship. Sir Samuels Wine Bar was rearranged into a Godiva Chocolate Cafe, while a new photo gallery was built on Deck 2.

Structural alterations were also carried out with the creation of thirty new Britannia Club cabins in a block added to Deck 13. Despite this additional bulk, which visibly increased the dimensions of the ship, *QM2*'s gross tonnage actually decreased to 149,215 due to the loss of the large open deck space that once occupied this area.

Further changes included the addition of six single ocean view cabins, created on Deck 3L in an area originally utilised by the Photo

Irish President Michael D. Higgins made a moving speech in honour of those who lost their lives aboard *Lusitania* and the people of Cobh who went to the aid of survivors. (Frame/Cross)

Queen Victoria alongside on Cobh. Passengers and crew attended the memorial service ashore as part of the Lusitania Remembered Voyage. (Frame/Cross)

▶ DID YOU KNOW?

In 2015 a copy of the *Magna Carta* was put on display aboard *QM2* and *Queen Victoria* to celebrate its 800th anniversary. In 1946 Cunard's flagship *Queen Elizabeth* transported one of the original copies of the Magna Carta back to Southampton. It had been moved to America for safe keeping during the First World War.

Queen Mary 2 and *Queen Elizabeth* as seen from *Queen Victoria* in May 2015. (Frame/Cross)

Captain Nick Bates reflects on what it takes to be a Captain:

In the early '80s Cunard Line came up with the hugely successful marketing ploy where passengers could fly one way on Concorde and return the other on board the *QE2*, this program was enhanced with onboard lectures from Concorde pilots and technical staff, always very popular and well attended.

This led to the idea that it would be wonderful if it could be arranged for the two great ships — if you could call Concorde a ship — to communicate with each other mid Atlantic.

Plans were put into operation including the placing of specialised communication equipment onboard the *QE2*. The captain at the time was Lawrence Portet, a wonderful man with an extremely dry sense of humour.

With all the equipment in place, a date and a time was set up when Concorde would be passing over *QE2* mid Atlantic. The team on the Bridge were nervous but eagerly tried to contact Concorde. After about 30 minutes or so we did indeed establish contact and Captain Portet was immediately informed.

On arriving on the Bridge he picked up the microphone and commenced this historic conversation. At the same time this conversation was being relayed to our 1,750 passengers and to the passengers onboard Concorde.

After a brief introduction Captain Portet asked what their guests were doing to while away their short trip. Immediately the Concorde pilot explained that the cabin crew were in the process of serving lunch and went on to give a very detailed description of everything that was being served.

At that point just about the entire Bridge team realised that the Concorde pilot was bound to ask what we were serving our guests for their lunch. Knowing Captain Portet didn't have a clue, a second officer was dispatched to the nearest restaurant, the Queens Grill, to get a menu.

Inevitably when the Concorde pilot finished reading out his menu, he asked what we were serving our guests by way of lunch. Sadly our messenger had failed to return and those on the Bridge wondered what on earth Captain Portet was going to say.

Without a moment's hesitation Captain Portet said that he would love to read out our menu, but feared that by the time he had finished Concorde would be landing in New York.

Many of us listening on the Bridge wondered if we could have thought of such an off-the-cuff response.

Gallery, while the Casino was rearranged to allow for an additional nine single cabins.

But perhaps the most talked about change took place in the Grand Lobby. Here, the glass elevators were removed, which greatly opened up the space and provided room for a welcoming meeting space to be created. This change was supplemented by the installation of striking starburst carpets; a design inspired by the original *Queen Mary*.

In 2017, Cunard expanded their itineraries further when the line sent *Queen Victoria* into the Amazon River. Notable for being the largest ship to transit the waterway at the time, the voyage has since been repeated, and remains a popular itinerary for *Queen Victoria*.

Following the success of QM2's refit, Cunard announced *Queen Victoria* would receive her own large-scale refurbishment. Undertaken in late May and early June 2017 at the Fincantieri shipyard in Palermo, Sicily, work included the addition of a new block of cabins to the ship's stern.

This addition increased *Queen Victoria*'s passenger capacity to over 2,000 passengers, but came at the cost of the ship's aft profile, which now appears boxier than originally designed.

In July 2017, *Queen Elizabeth* made headlines when she rendezvoused with the Royal Navy's new Aircraft Carrier *HMS Queen Elizabeth*. The meeting, off the coast of Scotland, was all the more significant as both ships had been named and christened by HM The Queen.

September 2017 marked the fiftieth Anniversary of the QE2's launch. In honour of this historic event, a special celebratory voyage was hosted aboard *Queen Elizabeth*. During the seventeen-night Mediterranean cruise, various guest speakers shared the long and illustrious history

QM2 was given an extensive refurbishment in 2016. One of the features of the remastered ship is the Carinthia Lounge on Deck 7. This space was formerly the Winter Garden. (Frame/Cross)

Queen Elizabeth's 2018 refurbishment included updates to the cabin decor and bedding. (Frame/Cross)

On 7 March 2019 *Queen Elizabeth* made her maiden call to Port Arthur in Tasmania, Australia. (Frame/Cross)

Queen Elizabeth has spent extended periods in Australian waters, with the ship regularly calling at Circular Quay, Sydney. (Frame/Cross)

'John Jenkins joined Cunard in 1934. He worked on the *Mauretania* from 1934 until her scrapping, then joined the RMS *Alaunia* until the outbreak of the Second World War. In 2019 he was celebrated as Cunard's oldest living crew member. His story is shared by friend Matthew Bambury:

I shared a room with eight men, I was the only bellboy in the room and it was a bit strange being in a room with eight fully grown men but it was just the way of it and that was that.

All crew quarters were referred to as glory holes and mine was positioned above the propellers so it was extremely noisy. My first few nights onboard the *Mauretania* I couldn't sleep but by the time we arrived in New York and the engines shut down, I couldn't sleep for the two nights we spent in the city, as it was just too quiet.

Eating in the crew quarters meant standing up and eating. I never had time to sit down and eat. At 5 a.m. I would be woken, have a quick but hearty breakfast standing up and then I would head up on deck to scrub a section of the decks clean. Then I was ordered back down to wash and get into my smart uniform and then make my way back up so I could perform my main job, opening the first-class dining saloon doors for breakfast, lunch and dinner.

I loved the dining room it was my favourite room onboard. It was beautiful; no two pieces of wood were the same. It was very impressive to look at and I remember how impressed the passengers used to be the first time they would see it. She was old by then but still a beautiful ship. For dinner I would have to wait until the last passengers had left. Then the head waiter would make me help clean up, by taking some of the cold fruit back down to the cold stores. I was always so hungry by that point that I used to pinch an apple from the fruit bowl, but my uniform was so well fitted that I could never really fit it in my pocket. But that never stopped me from having one!

I remember being sat in New York in between trips and one of the crew had a radio. We all sat around the radio and listened to the launch of the Cunarder '534' *Queen Mary*. I saw many ships when docked in New York, usually next to us were the *Berengaria* and *Aquitania*. Then down to piers 59 was normally the *Majestic* and *Olympic*. I can also remember the first time I arrived in New York in 1934 a large liner over the water berthed in Hoboken, one of the other crew said to me of that old girl, 'that's the *Leviathan*, she's heading off to scrap'.'

of *QE2*, with notable guests including Captain Ian McNaught and Commodore Ron Warwick.

At the same time as *QE2*'s fiftieth anniversary celebration was underway; two significant stories broke in the world media.

The first related to *QE2*'s future with rumours having circulated for weeks that work was underway to finally convert the ship into a floating hotel.

Later confirmed to be true, *QE2* opened in March 2018 with much of her Cunard interior intact. Changes include improvements to her cabins as well as the redesign of the Lido restaurant and new carpeting in her major public spaces.

The second major announcement came from Cunard, when they revealed their intention to build a new ship. At around 113,000 gt, the ship was named *Queen Anne*, and is set to join the fleet in May 2024.

Built at Fincantieri in Italy, artists' impressions of the vessel show a profile based on Holland America's Pinnacle Class. While smaller than *QM2*, the new ship is expected to hold close to 3,000 passengers – giving it the highest passenger capacity within the Cunard fleet.

In 2018, Cunard invested in upgrading *Queen Elizabeth* in preparation for her 2019 season. While smaller in scale than the refits aboard *QM2* and *Queen Victoria*, this refit was notable as it took place in Brest, France, a location that had not completed refurbishment work on the Cunard Queens before.

2,000 workers completed a series of enhancements, which included the re-carpeting of much of the ship, as well as structural enhancements to the Spa and shopping promenade.

In December 2018, *Queen Elizabeth* sailed from Southampton bound for Australia. Upon her arrival, she commenced the longest Cunard

Queen Elizabeth and *Costa Deliziosa* alongside in Barcelona, Spain. Both ships are variants of Carnival Corporation's Vista class. (Frame/Cross)

Commodore John Burton-Hall reflects on QE2's 1994 refit:

Refits are the most unromantic periods of a ship's life. QE2's 1994 refit in Hamburg has been more than well-documented. Looking back twenty-five years later I recall not just the major aspects of it, but my own personal trivia. When the ship first arrived I became reacquainted with a senior dockyard manager who invited me to dine with him. On the menu were eels from the River Elbe. This is something I have great difficulty eating and honesty would have been by far the best policy. However, manners dictated appreciation, which unfortunately condemned me to a weekly dinner of eel to maintain a healthy relationship with the dockyard management.

Every night at sea, in port and in dry-dock we maintain a fire watch consisting of a Clock Patrol reporting to the Officer of the Watch. Near the end of the refit, due to the volume of work being undertaken, night and day, I felt my presence on board 24/7 would be supportive to the Officer of the Watch, who had no reason to communicate this to the Clock Patrol. Unfortunately, when the Clock Patrol, on entering the Captain's dayroom, found an unconscious body in a boiler suit on a sofa, he was convinced that an unauthorised person had gained access to 'the holy of holies' and all hell broke loose.

During refits, one's personal life is reduced to basics, which take on disproportionate significance; such as the sanitary arrangement when the water goes off. Buckets are distributed. As Captain, I had my own personal bucket – rank has its privileges! The recipient of my phone call when I realised that this important piece of kit had been purloined was probably rather puzzled to receive this as deeply distressing news!

Australian season since the *Cunard Crown Monarch*'s itineraries in the mid-1990s.

In March 2019, the ship sailed north for Japan before sailing east to re-establish Cunard's presence in Alaska. These voyages were heavily booked, with the *Queen Elizabeth* the first Cunarder to sail in this region since *Cunard Crown Dynasty* was withdrawn from service over twenty years earlier. The popularity of *Queen Elizabeth*'s Australian, Japanese and Alaskan itineraries led to it being expanded in 2020.

In November 2019, *QM2* departed Southampton in celebration of Cunard's centenary in Southampton. The voyage marked the anniversary of Cunard relocating its express transatlantic services to the Hampshire city, with *Mauretania* inaugurating the route on 18 November 1919. During *QM2*'s voyage to New York, a special Sea City Museum exhibit was carried aboard, showcasing Cunard's connection to Southampton.

As 2019 drew to a close, Cunard prepared to enter its 180th year. 2020 represents eighteen decades since Sir Samuel Cunard established the first regularly scheduled transatlantic crossings.

This service paved the way for a travel revolution that has touched the lives of millions. Cunard has been involved in technological advancement and feats of engineering. It played a key role in the mass movement of immigrants in search of a new life and answered the call-to-arms in defence of Britain.

And despite the immense challenges of its 180th year, Cunard endured. It survived the Covid Pandemic, emerging ready to welcome its first new ship in over a decade.

Today, over 65,700 days since its formation, Cunard still offers regularly scheduled transatlantic crossings by ocean liner. It was the first line to offer this service, and today, 180 years later, it is the last – something Sir Samuel Cunard would undoubtedly be proud of.

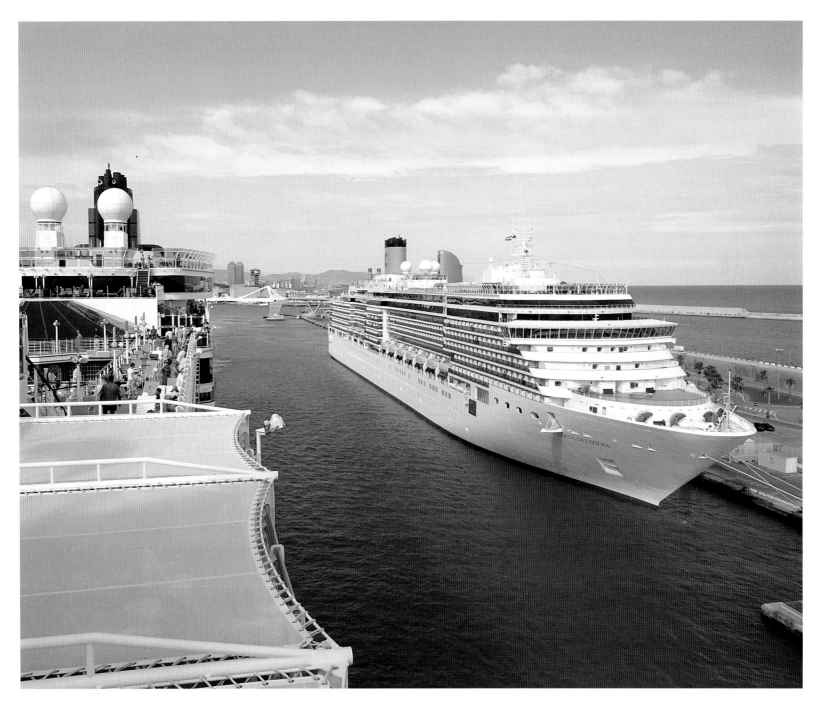

Costa Deliziosa and *Queen Elizabeth* were both built by Fincantieri and were both completed in 2010. (Frame/Cross)

Far Left: *QM2*'s Grand Lobby was given a striking new look, with the addition of a starburst carpet design, inspired by the art deco theme aboard the original *Queen Mary*. (Frame/Cross)

Left: One of the most significant alterations to *Queen Victoria* during her 2017 refit was the creation of the Britannia Club Restaurant in a space once occupied by the Chart Room Bar. (Frame/Cross)

> ### Commodore John Burton-Hall recalls shipboard life during the Gulf War:
>
> Even when a ship is in a war zone, normal mundane ship life continues. When I commanded *Cunard Princess* during the first Gulf War, we lay alongside in Bahrain for considerable periods of time. As evidenced by a phone call to my wife, I was gleefully anticipating the prospect of merely moving the ship around the jetty to another berth. This simple manoeuvre took our minds away from the stress of forty-nine scud attacks over the Bahrain area.

Queen Victoria's Winter Garden was given a bright colour palette during her 2017 refit. (Frame/Cross)

QM2 operates both transatlantic and cruise itineraries. During her cruises she visits many different ports, including the Italian port of Naples. (Frame/Cross)

Queen Victoria (pictured) and Queen Elizabeth operate year round cruise itineraries. While Queen Elizabeth has been spending long periods cruising far from home, Queen Victoria has largely focussed on the European market. (Frame/Cross)

QM2 calls Southampton home and is a regular visitor to the port. In 2019 she hosted the Cunard-Southampton centenary celebrations, which commemorated 100 years of Cunard using the port as its UK hub. (Frame/Cross)

Queen Victoria's wraparound boat deck offers a great view of the ship's wake. (Frame/Cross)

AFTERWORD

by Captain Aseem A. Hashmi MNM

Famous shipping Lines have come and gone over the decades, the likes of the Shaw Saville Line, the Union Castle Line and of course the famous White Star Line. But there is one Line that has stood the test of time and is one of the oldest names to have graced its presence on the oceans, particularly the North Atlantic Ocean and that is the esteemed Cunard Line.

The Cunard Line has survived and literally weathered the storm for the past 180 years, not due to the Line's vintage, but because the company has always looked into the future, whilst questioning the present and celebrating the past and this is still very true today. It was at the age of 52 that Sir Samuel Cunard embarked on his North Atlantic venture, quite an advanced age in the nineteenth century. Sir Samuel was a man of both vision and tremendous courage and the famous phrase coined by President John F. Kennedy over a century later with respect to manned expeditions to the moon – 'we choose to go to the moon … not because it's easy, but because its hard' – could easily be applied to Sir Samuel's logic in 1840.

Over the past 180 years the Cunard Line has pioneered numerous maritime achievements that the marine industry takes for granted today. It was the Cunard Line in 1848 that established the system of navigation lights (red to port and green to starboard), which all ships and aircraft use today. In 1881 the *Servia* was the first steel passenger ship in the world to have electricity, while the *Campania* was the first ship to have wireless communication in 1901. During times of conflict the Cunard Line has unfailingly always answered the call to duty, from the Crimean War in 1854 to the first Gulf War in 1992. During the times of requisition, the company has suffered great material losses in terms of ships damaged and sunk, but also tremendous personal human cost. However, in 1912 there would have been an even greater human loss if it wasn't for the small Cunard ship *Carpathia*, which rushed through icy waters to rescue 705 survivors from the Titanic tragedy.

Whilst the Cunard Line has always tried to ride the crest of the wave, at times during its history it was at real risk of being over-oared and submerged economically, particularly with the onset of the

Queen Elizabeth alongside Circular Quay in Sydney Harbour during her 2019 Australian season. (Frame/Cross)

jet age. The company did not shy away from this new threat and even flirted with the idea of going into civil aviation with the creation of BOAC-Cunard Airways and later Cunard Eagle Airways, the former becoming British Airways as we know it today.

When I joined the Cunard Line as a cadet twenty-five years ago, the fleet comprised of fourteen vessels, including the Royal Viking Fleet, the Crown Fleet, Super Yachts *Sea Goddess I & II*, river cruising vessels and, of course, the then Flagship, the *QE2*. Today the company has three magnificent ships (with a fourth one on the blocks) and I have the privilege of being in command of one of them, the Flagship *Queen Mary 2*. I believe all of us of who have and have had the honour of serving in the Cunard Line and the millions of passengers who have graced the decks of the company's liners past and present are a significant detail in the 180-year-old tapestry that is the Cunard Line. We are caretakers of this legacy in this moment in time and when the time comes we will pass the mantel and the Line onto future generations and I have no doubt that sometime in the future Sir Samuel's Cunard Line will have another 180 years to serve and celebrate.

I congratulate Chris Frame and Rachelle Cross on this most fitting tribute to the Cunard Line in this special 180-year anniversary edition which meticulously documents 'our' journey so far for all to relive, enjoy and treasure for the future … Bon Voyage!

Captain Aseem A. Hashmi MNM
Master on RMS *Queen Mary 2*

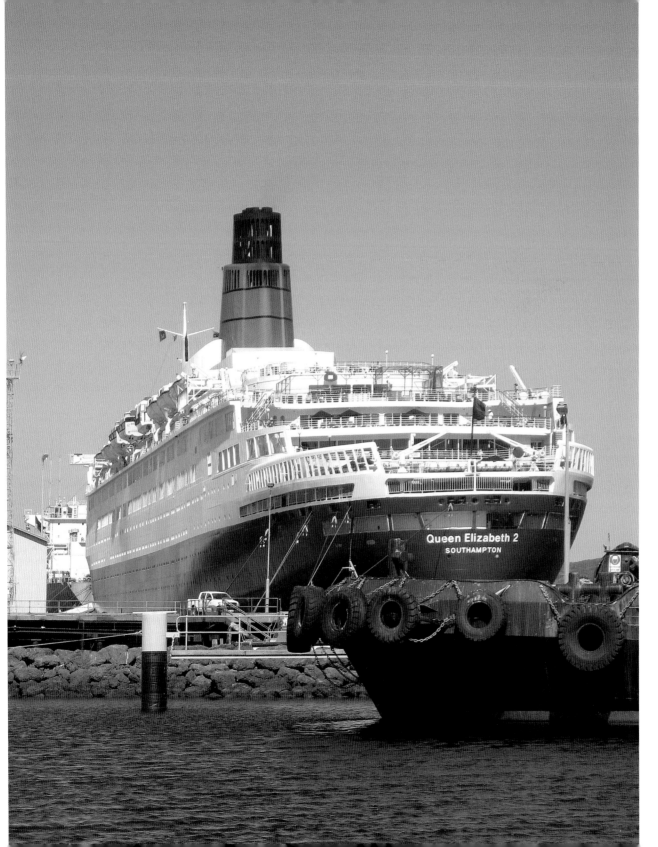

QE2 berthed at Albany during her farewell world cruise in 2008. (Frame/Cross)

BIBLIOGRAPHY

Books and Articles

Braynard, F.O. and Miller, W.H., *Picture History of the Cunard Line* (Dover; United Kingdom, 1991).

Britton, A., *RMS Mauretania* (The History Press; United Kingdom, 2013).

Chirnside, M., *Aquitania: The Ship Beautiful* (The History Press; United Kingdom, 2009).

De Kerbrech, R., *Ships of the White Star Line* (Ian Allen Publishing; United Kingdom, 2009).

Dickens, C., *American Notes: John W. Lovell & Co.* (New York; United States, 1842). Source: Archive.org.

Frame, C. and Cross, R., *The Evolution of the Transatlantic Liner* (The History Press; United Kingdom, 2013).

Frame, C. and Cross, R., *The Cunard Story* (The History Press; United Kingdom, 2010).

Frame, C. and Cross, R., *The QE2 Story* (The History Press; United Kingdom, 2009).

Gandy, M., 'The Britannia Cup', *The Antiques Magazine*, Vol. 122 (July 1982), pp. 156–58.

Grant, R.G., *Flight: The Complete History* (Dorling Kindersley Limited; United Kingdom, 2007).

Harding, S. Gray, *Ghost: The RMS Queen Mary at War* (Pictorial Histories Publishing Company; United States of America, 1982).

Harvey, C. and Cartwright, R., *The Saga Sisters* (The History Press; United Kingdom, 2006).

Hutchings, D.F., *RMS Queen Elizabeth – From Victory to Valhalla* (Kingfisher Publications; United Kingdom, 1990).

Langley, J.G., *Steam Lion: A Biography of Samuel Cunard* (Brick Tower Press; United States of America, 2006).

Maxtone-Graham, J. and Lloyd, H., *Queen Mary 2: The Greatest Ocean Liner of Our Time* (Bulfinch; United Kingdom, 2004).

McCutcheon, J., *Cunard: A Photographic History* (Tempus; United Kingdom, 2004).

Miller, W.H., *Pictorial Encyclopedia of Ocean Liners 1860–1994* (Dover; United Kingdom, 1995).

Miller, W.H., *Picture History of British Ocean Liners: 1900 to the Present* (Dover; United Kingdom, 2001).

Miller, W.H., *Picture History of the Queen Mary and Queen Elizabeth* (Dover; United Kingdom, 2001).

Miller, W.H., SS *United States: Speed Queen of the Seas* (Amberley Publishing; United Kingdom, 2010).

Osborne, B.D. and Armstrong, R., *Scotland's Greatest Ships* (Luthan Press Ltd; United Kingdom, 2007).

Plisson, P., *Queen Mary 2: The Birth of a Legend: Harry. N* (Abrams; United Kingdom, 2004).

Warwick, R.W., *QE2: The Cunard Line Flagship Queen Elizabeth II* (Norton; United Kingdom, 1999).

Warwick, S. and Roussel, M., *Shipwrecks of the Cunard Line* (The History Press; United Kingdom, 2012).

Williams, D., *Cunard's Legendary Queens of the Seas* (Ian Allen Publishing; United Kingdom, 2004).

Wills, E., *The Fleet, 1840–2004: Cunard's Floating Palaces from the Earliest Days of Steam to Queen Mary 2* (The Open Agency; United Kingdom, 2004).

Film

Queen Mary Launch, c. 1934.

Queen Elizabeth Launch, c. 1939.

The Great Ships television series, various episodes (Perpetual Motion Films).

The Liners television series, various episodes (Demand DVD).

Personal Conversations

Commodore R.W. Warwick.
Commodore C. Rynd.
Commodore J. Burton-Hall.
Captain I. McNaught.
Director PR, Cunard Rachel Lloyd.
Captain N. Bates.
Cunard Historian, M. Gallagher.

Company Documents

Cunard Line, On-board Promotional Material (various versions), 2009.
Cunard Line, Queen Mary 2: Technical and Bridge Facts (Various Versions), 2009.
Cunard Line, Media Releases (various) sourced from www.cunard.com and Way Back Machine in 2019.

Websites (General)

Chris Frame's Cunard Page: www.chriscunard.com
Cunard's Official Website: www.cunard.com

Websites (Specific)

Archives Today: archive.today – Navies in Transition. Accessed 19 July 2014.
Clydesite: www.clydesite.co.uk – Cunard Cargo Ship Database at Clydesite.
Genealogy website: rmhh.co.uk – RMS Andria pages at Hall Genealogy website.
The Lusitania Resource: www.rmslusitania.info – Lusitania in the war.
Marconi Website: www.marconigraph.com – Includes historical notes.
Rob Lightbody's QE2 website: www.roblightbody.com – Queen Elizabeth 2.
Daily Mail: www.dailymail.co.uk – 'End of an Era as Iconic QE2 sold for scrap'. Accessed 20 June 2014.
Source News: www.soue.org.uk – Turbinia information.

Newspapers

Author unknown, 'Takeover offer for Cunard planned by Trafalgar House', Montreal Gazette, 2 July 1971.
Author unknown, 'Cunard Chief Resigns', Herald Scotland, 21 September 1996.
Cowell, A., 'Belfast Shipyard Loses Bid to Build Queen Mary 2, and Many Jobs', New York Times, 11 March 2000.
Granger Blair, W., 'B.O.A.C. buys out Cunard's share; $32.2-Million price to help ship line offset losses', The New York Times, 16 September 1966, pp. 55.
Ipsen, E., 'Kværner is Close to Bidding for Troubled Group: Lifeline for Trafalgar House?', The New York Times, 28 February 1996.
Jones, S., 'QE2 sold to become Floating Hotel', Travel Weekly, 18 June 2007.
McDowell, E., 'Chief's Strategy for Ailing Cruise Line', The New York Times, 6 August 1996.

For Further Reading

If you're interested in the history of other ocean liners written by Chris Frame and Rachelle Cross, take a look at:

The QM2 Story.
The QE2 Story.

QM2: A Photographic Journey.
QE2: A Photographic Journey.
Queen Victoria: A Photographic Journey.
Queen Elizabeth: A Photographic Journey.

A Photographic History of P&O Cruises.
A Photographic History of the Orient Line.

Photographic/Bibliographical Notice

All images used within this book are reproduced with the express permission of the photograph/collection owner. All images are referenced as such. Copyright and ownership of the images remain with the photograph owner/collection owner/photographer.

Every effort has been made to reference information correctly. Where information was found digitally, every effort was made to reference the original source.

Any bibliographic errors or omissions will be remedied in future editions.